YOU ARE THE PRODUCT

YOU ARE THE PRODUCT

HOW TO SURVIVE—AND THRIVE—IN THE ERA OF REPUTATION ECONOMICS

JOSHUA KLEIN

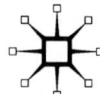
First published in hardcover in 2013 by PALGRAVE MACMILLAN® in the
United States—a division of St. Martin's Press LLC, 175 Fifth Avenue,
New York, NY 10010.

Palgrave® and Macmillan® are registered trademarks in the United States,
the United Kingdom, Europe and other countries.

ISBN: 978–1–137–27996–5 (paperback)

The Library of Congress has cataloged the hardcover edition as follows:

Klein, Joshua, 1974–
     Reputation economics : why who you know is worth more than what
you have / Joshua Klein.
       pages cm
     ISBN 978–1–137–27862–3 (hardback)
       1. Electronic commerce—Social aspects. 2. Marketing—Social aspects.
     3. Internet marketing—Social aspects. 4. Reputation—Economic aspects.
     5. Online social networks—Economic aspects. 6. Business networks—
     Social aspects. 7. Economics—Social aspects. I. Title.

HF5548.32.K576 2013
650.1'3—dc23   2013020565

A catalogue record of the book is available from the British Library.

Design by Newgen Knowledge Works (P) Ltd., Chennai, India.

First Palgrave Macmillan Trade paperback edition: March 2015

10 9 8 7 6 5 4 3 2 1

Printed in the United States of America.

To my aunts Jill, Yvonne, and Sharon: for teaching me that together, our differences can be our greatest strengths.

CONTENTS

ACKNOWLEDGMENTS

'd like to thank my wife, for supporting me in finishing this book while being beautifully pregnant throughout, and my son Óðinn, for making the deadline for the manuscript so abundantly clear. Similar thanks go to my family (on both continents) for being endlessly supportive and for constantly fielding weird questions. I'd particularly like to thank my test readers for their feedback, and especially David Goldstein for his careful (and comprehensive) edits. Of course, great thanks go to the many folks I interviewed, without whom this book wouldn't have been possible. As always, much thanks go to my agent, Mollie Glick, and all the smart folks at Palgrave Macmillan. Finally, my biggest thanks go to you, the reader—I hope we get to connect soon.

CHAPTER 1
WHAT IS YOUR MOTHER WORTH?

OPENING SHOTS ON THE FINANCIAL OLIGARCHY

During the 9/11 attacks in New York City, federal investigators were certain that the terrorists had used the black market and a network of friend-of-a-friend connections to covertly move the funds they needed. In truth, they used an FDIC-insured bank based in Florida. At the same time, foreign workers the world over whose earnings could spell literal life or death for *their* families back home transferred their funds using the same underground network the FBI was worried about the terrorists using—because they felt it was safer.

As part of the exact same trend, someone is tweeting more than 45 times a day *right now* so they can get upgraded to an executive suite the next time they book a room at a hotel. Someone else is spending hours and hours after work painstakingly answering other people's technical questions, for free, without ever having a use for the solutions themselves. Neither of them is getting paid for this work, and yet they each consider this a significant career investment.

What's going on here? What's the connection, and what does this have to do with reputation, or the new world order of technology?

This book answers those questions. It is a guide to how the present moment in history is in the eye of a very peculiar storm, a deeply indrawn breath by the collective population of our tiny blue and gray planet before we jump into the next stage of global commerce. It's about destroying the unnatural assumption that financial currencies (and their related banking, loan, credit, and other services) are the pinnacle of human commercial development, and not an artifact of a time before the internet. It's about how we're beginning to stop pretending, as a species, that it's normal or even preferable to use money as our sole system of exchange.

This is happening thanks to an influx of powerful new methods of computer intelligence, sensor networks, and social platforms that are just beginning to shake the existing world of financial commerce in favor of a more human form of regulation and currency: reputation.

In the process, our expectations of otherwise ancient methods of exchange—and the technologies now encapsulating them—are leaving us woefully unprepared for the markets that are emerging. Businesses are flailing as they're subsumed by competitors created literally overnight in garages and basements. Traditional models of exchange are being undercut by the sudden appearance of cryptocurrencies like Bitcoin. Marketing and political campaigns backed by extensive customer research are falling flat as those "customers" suddenly vanish into crowdsourced purchasing mechanisms. Entire product categories are eroding into person-to-person exchanges backed by broad, cheap online platforms. At its extreme, consumer groups are starting to appear with the sole purpose of obviating entire markets, armed with the technology, relationships, and networks to actually do so.

Those are just the changes we're seeing in the First World. Meanwhile, the existing financial system that's been so preeminent as a commercial method here has set us up to be seriously blindsided as the rest of the world evolves. While we've been toiling away since the industrial revolution under the illusion that money is the only way to exchange value, the rest of the globe has been getting around their own exchange problems in other ways, often with no participation in financial mechanisms like loans, credit cards, or bank accounts at all. The result is an enormous global network of overlapping markets, trust relationships, unregulated commerce systems, and mixed currencies, every one of which is uniquely derived to represent the individual valuations of its participants.

Until now this rich diversity of methods has languished under the usual panoply of Second World and Third World market problems: communication restrictions, price discovery issues, missing transaction mechanisms, et cetera—all of which made them generally much less efficient than the existing global banking network. And until very recently that was all there was to it.

At the same time, the global technological elite have enjoyed the advent of platforms such as Facebook and Twitter and started finding ways to connect, person to person, at a whole new scale. Then, as the financial systems we relied on became unable to support these platforms, we started implementing workarounds for new kinds of exchanges of our own: cryptocurrencies like Bitcoin to enable more anonymous payments online; eBay seller ratings to allow strangers to buy from strangers with confidence; sites where peers rate each other's ability to answer questions germane to their field, resulting in better job prospects for those who rise within the meritocracy; self-aggregating car services to help people find a cab when their city's "official" taxi monopoly fails to meet demand.

Suddenly, there are a whole variety of emerging marketplaces available to us, all of which use this new, wide web of social networks and the reputation they engender as currency in part of the exchange. This isn't new as a mechanism—it's how most of the world does, and has always done, its business. What's really changed is that for the first time all the limiting factors that have kept these methods underground are being freed of their restrictions of scope and scale. The Internet is just now shaking off a primitive monopoly of financial exchange to allow people to exchange with all the multitudes of methods they have used for most of human existence. The result is massive opportunity in the form of new markets—and an incredible destructive force as consumers begin circumventing traditional business models entirely.

This confluence of global evolution, technically, socially, and economically, is setting us up to either take a terrible fall or make an incredible evolution (or both). The World Wide Web is becoming truly worldwide, and the openness of data and new platforms, and the resistance to regulation and control that are literally coded into them, will rework everything we know about commerce. Just as the twitterati and foreign workers of the world already know—and the 9/11 terrorists carefully avoided—a person's reputation can function as a far more powerful and effective means of ensuring a person's welfare than the machinations of massive, deeply bureaucratic, and highly impersonal institutions. That enlightened self interest is about to reshape commerce as we know it, particularly as the slumbering third world begins to onramp into the technology platforms and exchange systems we're creating in the first via the web.

Welcome...to Reputation Economics.

THE STATUS QUO IN A DISRUPTIVE ECOLOGY

So what *are* reputation economies? It's actually pretty straightforward—they're exchanges that use more (or other) measures than just financial currency. If you've ever participated in a white elephant gift exchange, you've done it. If you've given a birthday gift, or owed someone a favor, or hired a friend of a friend, you've done it. Reputation economics isn't a new form of exchange—it's how commerce traditionally happened before the industrial era got its collective panties in a bunch and decided that everything under the sun had to be fungible for cash.

Money is a great idea (we have the industrial revolution to thank for it, among other things), but human beings aren't reductionist enough to turn everything into cash value. After all, what's your mom worth? That's not a trick question, by the way. It's a serious inquiry that you might be asked by a life insurance adjustor, a retirement community manager, or even a Mother's Day gift card site. It assumes that all the elements of our lives that play a part in any human exchange—what your values are, who you know, what resources you have—can all be boiled down to money alone.

Like any apples-and-oranges equation, this doesn't hold up in real life. Sure, it works well enough—we just offload any externalities by pretending that things like reputation, relationships, or motivations aren't part of how commerce works. And because everyone plays along, the financial system staggers forward. (For most of us, anyway.)

But the truth is, you can't put a market price on love or happiness or loyalty; it's incredibly difficult to quantify relationships. Reputation is the closest thing we have for facilitating transactions, because reputation itself is tied to context, which means it's inherently and relatively qualitative instead of quantitative. It also means you need adequate context for it to hold water. As an alternative, finance's assumption that you can take a relationship and boil it down to a number is insanely reductionist...but this is the assumption that for a long time was the best we had for facilitating commerce, particularly at scale.

This assumption about how commerce should happen isn't singularly necessary anymore. In fact, in many cases it isn't even desirable, because it results in most of us leaving value on the table. For example, if I own a bunch of sheep and harvest their wool, I can sell that wool on the open market for price X. But that doesn't take into account that my good friend, the one whom I spent three days in January helping bail out his flooded basement, might want to buy the wool for the much greater price of Y. Or that my sister, who I forgot to buy a birthday present for, might really enjoy the wool as a gift, which is worth something else entirely and is difficult to measure in dollars, yen, or euros. Again, what is your mother worth?

Reputation economies are systems of exchange that account for the fact that different people value different things in different ways at different times. Often, financial exchanges are embedded inside reputation ones; when I tip my server well because he or she went out of their way to help me, I'm acting on our relationship in addition to paying the pre-established market price. The difference is that reputation economies don't *require* financial systems to operate. That's eye opening to most, and threatening to many. It's also an *opportunity*—organizations that recognize this stand to quickly evolve leaps and bounds ahead of their competitors as reputation becomes more fluidly embedded in all our transactions.

After all, when I buy a cup of coffee at Walmart, both Walmart and I know what it's worth in dollars and cents, which is a function of what the market will bear—a set price established by the "invisible hand" of market demand and product supply. Ideally, this results in the optimal price for both buyer and seller. But when I drop by my aunt's place and she offers me a cup of coffee and then asks for help getting her car started, we don't pull out a pad of paper to deduct auto repair from coffee prices. Why not? Because that's not how human beings really work. We don't need to look up the market price of coffee or auto repair, because our brains are hardwired to take into account a plethora of dynamic, contextualized factors in order to valuate both services non-financially.

Again, all of this wouldn't matter much if it weren't for the Internet coming along and disrupting everything by allowing anyone on the planet to connect directly with anybody else. As a result of that massive change in scope, we're now able to have virtual cups of coffee with or to provide digitized auto repair for anyone, anywhere. More significantly, it also lets us get enough context, instantly, to make the same evaluation about otherwise complete strangers that we do about our aunt. If anything, the shift toward a prevalence of virtual (or virtualized) goods and services means we have even *more* context to make our valuations by. And increasingly, these platforms are available for real-world goods and services as well.

As an example, if I need someone to help me mod my IKEA furniture, I can use Freelancer.com to learn everything I need to about a potential designer in order to figure out exactly what the work is worth based on his or her reputation. And he or she can learn enough about me to figure out what they're comfortable charging me, as opposed to anybody else on the planet. Better yet, we can decide to trade work, favors, online account access, wool, rap songs, or anything else we want instead of or in addition to cash, and the pricing is identically negotiated. Again, it's an intuitive exchange based on reputation, except that whereas in the past I could have made this exchange only with the people in my village, I now have more than 7 billion people to work with. Even more importantly, I now have an exploding number of platforms whose sole purpose is to validate, authenticate, and support communities of individuals' reputations for any such exchange. Freelancer is one, but there are markets for borrowing cars, taking classes, or sharing tips on your cancer treatments that simply didn't exist before, with more appearing all the time. It's as though an eBay seller rating suddenly appeared for everyone online for anything anyone ever offered on any platform.

The fact that this is becoming available to anyone on the globe is critical, because reputation economies work well for person-to-person exchanges (i.e., those involving discrete human beings, like you or me) but not so much for big established bureaucracies whose advantages of scale rely on interacting with "customers." This isn't because companies can't have a reputation—indeed, what else is brand than a publicized reputation? Instead, it's because companies can't have personal relationships and therefore cannot enjoy the kind of trust two people can establish between each other. I.e., if my cable company screws up my billing, who is the individual I should hold responsible? The result is that all the nonfinancial elements of an exchange that could otherwise be enabled by trust simply don't exist for the purposes of a corporate transaction.

After all, the fact that Walmart needs to charge the same price for a cup of coffee in every store in Michigan in order to maintain adequate supply chains, management overhead, market competitiveness, et cetera, just doesn't matter to me. As individuals, we couldn't really give a damn; we already *know* what our aunt's cup of coffee is worth to us and whether it's worth helping her get her car started or if we'd rather come up with some excuse to get out of it. That doesn't help Walmart at all. If anything, it's a big problem when customers start expecting to have hyperpersonalized relationship-based price evaluations for every transaction in every Walmart store. After all, any sizable organization with the standard arrangement of phone trees and customer scripts and offshore support staff *can't* create meaningful human relationships with you—the cost in paying the salaries and retraining enough individuals to responsibly act on the company's behalf would be prohibitive. It would require radically changing the entire corporate structure. Instead, at best, it can create an unspoken, semi-legal commercial relationship with you which will last exactly as long as the company does what you're willing to pay money for…and no further.

Ostensibly this should work in our favor. And eventually it will, because the majority of us aren't going to keep playing a game that's rigged against us forever. After all, if I help a Walmart employee fix a flat in the parking lot, they still have to charge me the normal price for my coffee. If he or she "forgets" to charge me for it, that's a loss as far as Walmart is concerned—and so it's a punishable offense.

This has worked just fine for a while now. Most businesses are sitting within a system of exchange that works very well at their level of scope, scale, and control. So far, it's a position that's being enhanced by emerging technologies. Despite the suddenly super-human ability to network with anyone on the planet that many of us are enjoying, at this stage most of the cards are being held by the entrenched financial and commercial systems—and they've got a really, really good hand.

That particular hand is so good because the platforms that we're all starting to lean on to get more value out of our non-financial resources are based on some pretty cool emerging technologies—stuff like cloud computing, data mining, sensor networks, and the like. The problem is that so far, only big companies are really mak-ing use of them. And they're investing a lot of time and money into these technologies in order to get more money out of all those afore-mentioned resources we're not currently realizing ourselves—stuff like our shopping habits, our friend networks, personal relation-ships, likes and dislikes, purchasing histories, plans for the future, skills and desires, and more. And they're getting pretty good at it, inasmuch as a brand can extract money from a customer.

But that's hitting a wall, which is exactly the point at which we see money failing to represent what's of value to us. That fail-ure is coming through reputation economies, because reputation economies rely on—among other things—personal trust. I trust in Coca-cola to provide me with a sugary beverage that will taste like I expect it to, just like I trust my mom to listen for a reason-able amount of time when I want to whine about my manuscript deadlines. But I would never, ever, *ever* offer a kidney to Coke no matter how poorly their stock prices plummet, whereas I'd pop one out for my mom in a heartbeat. That's the difference between reputation and financial economies, and it's what makes reputation economies so much richer, deeper, and more powerful. Reputation economies incorporate all the intangibles that make us human beings—the things that we value, not just the cash in our wallets—and that makes them forever beyond the reach of strictly financially bound institutions.

THE APPROACHING TECHNOLOGY TIPPING POINT

So what does that mean for commerce? How are these technologies changing things for normal people? And how does reputation play a role?

Reputation economics is simultaneously one of the oldest social methods for valuating goods or services and an entirely new set of technological means for conducting exchange based on same. From jobs (via potential employers looking us up online) to purchase ratings (via our browser history and online behaviors being tracked) to direct commerce (via people getting cheaper rates on services and products thanks to Klout.com ranking their popularity highly), reputation economics is becoming the new bugaboo of an increasingly pervasive online world. Privacy demarcates it. Authenticity predicates it. Our buying power is informed by it—and will soon be defined by it.

The breadcrumb trails of our online lives are being hoovered up and analyzed in quickly expanding circles of corporate partnerships by rapidly improving technologies. Our social behaviors on Facebook, in newsgroups or community forums, at the store via our discount cards, by our cell phone carriers tracking our movements, and more are being microscopically dissected, categorized, analyzed, and distributed. The result? Those companies looking to sell to us know before we do when we'll look to buy what, the maximum price we'll pay for a particular product at a particular time on a particular day, who we'll listen to for advice on a purchase, and when we're likely to ask them.

Here's a powerful example, and one that bears being spelled out. Back in 2009, Target approached one of its internal statisticians to see if he could identify when a woman was likely to get pregnant, even if she didn't want anyone to know. The reason is that one of the only times shoppers significantly alter their buying habits is during major lifestyle changes—and having a baby is the biggest. If you can attract a new customer around that time, you can convince them to start buying all kinds of *other* things at your store that they normally wouldn't, and to continue to do so as often as they need it. Because Target sells everything from groceries to bicycles, this makes expecting parents the holy grail of consumer acquisitions.

The trick, of course, is to get your marketing in before anyone else. Once a parent has a baby it becomes public record, and they get deluged with so much advertising it's effectively meaningless. To pull that trick off, Target collects as much data as it can about a particular consumer, whom it identifies by a "Guest ID." From a *New York Times Magazine* article:

> Linked to your Guest ID is demographic information like your age, whether you are married and have kids, which part of town you live in, how long it takes you to drive to the store, your estimated salary, whether you've moved recently, what credit cards you carry in your wallet and what Web sites you visit. Target can buy data about your ethnicity, job history, the magazines you read, if you've ever declared bankruptcy or got divorced, the year you bought (or lost) your house, where you went to college, what kinds of topics you talk about online, whether you prefer certain brands of coffee, paper towels, cereal, or applesauce, your political leanings, reading habits, charitable giving, and the number of cars you own.[1]

By analyzing all this data, Target is able to assign each shopper a "pregnancy prediction" score and, more importantly, estimate the woman's due date down to a very narrow window. This lets Target send coupons aimed at very specific stages of her pregnancy. Because Target has so much data attached to her Guest ID number, they frequently know how to trigger the woman's buying habits. For example, they might be able to predict that if she receives a coupon via e-mail she'll be prompted to make a purchase online, or if she gets a physical mailer at a certain time of week she'll use it on her weekly grocery shopping trip.

The problem with all this, of course, is that aside from the fact that exercising all this control is both enormously effective (and thereby profitable), *it is also very creepy*. But the results were too good to pass up, so Target had every intention of using them. The question then became how to use this information without letting the buyer know they were using it.

"We have the capacity to send every customer an ad booklet, specifically designed for them, that says, 'Here's everything you bought last week and a coupon for it,'" said one Target executive. "We do that for grocery products all the time."[2] The problem was that in this case Target's goal was to get them to shop for items they didn't even know they needed yet, because Target knew before they did what they were about to want to buy.

What Target did next is a classic example of the kind of error corporations are making in the age of reputation economics. Instead of making it clear what they were doing—coming clean to their consumers in order to earn their trust, and then finding ways to use their technical capacity to everyone's benefit—they tried to trick their customers.

"We started mixing in all these ads for things we knew pregnant women would never buy, so the baby ads looked random," said the same Target executive. "We'd put an ad for a lawn mower next to diapers. We'd put a coupon for wineglasses next to infant clothes. That way, it looked like all the products were chosen by chance. And we found out that as long as a pregnant woman thinks she hasn't been spied on, she'll use the coupons. She just assumes that everyone else on her block got the same mailer for diapers and cribs. As long as we don't spook her, it works."

Work it did—and well. Shortly after the new advertising campaign started, between 2002 and 2010, Target's revenues grew from $44 billion to $67 billion.

The problem, of course, is that eventually the secret got out. I've referenced this example numerous times in speaking engagements, and I almost always hear from people afterward who tell me they've stopped or intend to stop shopping at Target because of this. Full stop. The reason is that we don't *like* having the implied social contract of trust between buyers and sellers broken; I expect to be able to manage my reputation (and personal data) to the point at which I'm not being manipulated in ways unknown to me. I recognize that billboards and flyers and magazine ads are designed to change my opinion favorably toward products, and I accept that. But the concept that I can be tricked into producing a child as a byproduct of a company trying to hit its sales goals smacks of mind control. It's enough to turn people off from buying from a company entirely.

Target's not alone in playing this decidedly risky game; every multinational company—hell, every company with data to analyze, which is pretty much all of them—is currently in the market for data analysts. It's the sexiest new profession around, because it's enormously effective and can drive record profits. But as it does so, it risks alienating customers and raises the specter of privacy violations higher and higher in the public consciousness. At some point, something's going to break, and consumers will push back—with their wallets.

THE REVOLUTION WILL BE DIGITIZED

A big part of the problem is that this sort of godlike technological power isn't democratically distributed. It isn't even accurately applied. Every day someone with a high Klout score gets comped a room upgrade at a major hotel—even if their high Klout score was gained by posting YouTube videos of themselves trashing hotel rooms. A single mom is overcharged for a household product purchase because her online history indicates she'll be more tolerant of price gouging—because she's often purchased that same product at a higher quantity on behalf of a large company. Someone who has a hugely popular blog about environmental issues and carpooling is deluged with advertisements for gas-guzzling sports cars because they write under a pseudonym—and happen to be a 30-year-old white male.

That's the bad news; a lot of these capabilities just aren't being used well, and are often used for short-term profit at the expense of long-term gain. The good news is that those same tools and techniques can be used both more accurately and in ways that produce value for everyone involved.

For example, the emerging abundance economy can turn the traditional scarcity model on its head by using the powers of scope and scale offered by the internet for the first time in human history. What's an abundance economy? Basically, it used to be that if you had a thing and gave it to someone else, you didn't have it anymore. A sheep, a bushel of grain, your daughter—once someone else owned it, you didn't.

That's not true anymore. Now, if I write some software and give you a copy, I still own the software. In fact, if you give a copy to eight hundred billion other people, I still don't have the software any less. Instead, something interesting happens—all those people now have software I wrote, and they all know I wrote it, and (here's the kicker) *some of them might actually feel grateful for it.*

This results in all kinds of secondary effects, but the most significant is that suddenly, giving things away for free can offer a serious return. If I share a video on how to make pickles, I might get known as the best guy to go to about making pickles, which could really give a boost to my burgeoning pickle business. But it could also mean that a big pickle company might become aware of me and want to buy me out, or that cucumber growers near me might reach out with a great deal, or that a fan who really liked my pickles might simply write me a really nice letter thanking me.

That last one is an important point, by the way—not all returns are financial.

Regardless, the point remains that the abundance economy offers a variety of opportunities to benefit from giving things away where before there were none. All of a sudden, anything that can be shared online can produce an abundance of benefits that didn't exist previously in quantities large enough to be worth considering. Take Justin Bieber as an example—how many demo tapes would he have had to physically mail out to create enough fans to launch his career before YouTube existed?

Where this *really* gets interesting is when we consider that you can now exchange physical "things" over the Internet. Want that chair I've got in my living room? No problem—let me take a few pictures with my phone and send it to an online service that'll render it as a CAD design you can print with the 3D printer on your desk. I'm not joking; just google "3D print chair design" for a taste of the future of furniture.

This is one of the big effects of the abundance economy; the emergence of the primacy of design, where the commercial costs of an object are being increasingly abstracted away. Shipping? Being commodified by the rise in consumers ordering online instead of buying in stores. Manufacture? That cost is being decimated by new robotics technologies and distributed processing. Marketing? Increasingly, that's being done solely by word of mouth scaled across instant, global communication systems—no PR agency required.

Instead, the *cost* of an object lies increasingly in the creative process required to design it in the first place. Once that design exists, it can be—you guessed it—freely distributed. At which point we have the abundance economy all over again. The magic pixie dust known as the Internet just got blown hither and yon over commercial retail, and nothing will ever be the same again.

That's not the really exciting part, however. The fact that I can e-mail you a chair is cool, but it's still just a chair. The really far-reaching implications of reputation economics comes from the fact that, *as a means of exchange*, reputation exceeds financial methods in terms of potential return. Let's say that again—reputation economics can give you more value in an exchange than a purely financial transaction.

The abundance economy explanation above hints at why this is, but it goes deeper than the potential for free distribution. Why? Because reputation is something individuals intuitively use to valuate each other—*as* individuals—using a variety of currencies which can supply more value for both buyer and seller. Even more important, this intuitive valuation of relationships is how the majority of the world—by which I mostly mean the Second and Third Worlds—is more familiar conducting commerce. That fact alone makes reputation economics the single most critical, disruptive element for commerce, globally, going forward.

Not impressed? Consider this: As of this writing only 34.3 percent of the world has Internet access. That amount is up 566.4 percent in a little over the last decade and shows no sign of slowing.[3] The fastest-growing segment of that is mobile phones: 80 percent of the people in the world have a mobile phone right now, although out of the 5 billion mobile phones in the world, only 1.08 billion are smartphones—i.e., phones with Internet access.[4] Of those, over 50 percent of the smartphone penetration is in developed markets, with less than 20 percent in emerging markets.[5]

In other words, the markets that are most likely to make use of all these new reputation-based social networks and methods of exchange *haven't even arrived yet.* While we're twittering away about the miracle of funny cat videos on our phones, entrepreneurs in Senegal are soon to have all the same access to technology and capacity that we have. And when they do, they will approach it with reputation economies as their standard instead of "our" model of banks and loans and checks and mortgages.

It's a perfect storm of emerging technologies enabling widespread reputation assessment, analysis, and validation, coupled with powerful new methods of exchange which rely on models that are extraordinarily intuitive for how most of the world does commerce. And all this at exactly the same time as the bulk of the planet's population is just about to start conducting exchange online.

It's going to be a wild ride.

CHAPTER 2
A SHORT HISTORY OF MONEY

INTUITION + INTERNET = THE DEATH OF BANKING?

Computers are astoundingly good at a number of tasks, but anticipating human intuition isn't one of them. As computational capability extends globally, however, it *does* provide previously impossible scope and scale for commercial transactions of every kind. All of a sudden anyone can buy from or sell to anyone else on the planet.

That capability is intuitive. When you went to trade your handmade cheeses for a woven blanket in the village market, you made decisions about the exchange based on a variety of information about the person you were trading with. Intuitively, based on your own needs, what you knew about the other party, and your anticipated or desired outcome, you settled on an agreement for how much cheese each blanket is worth. Called "trade," it's a method of exchange common to every known configuration of human society.

When you take the leap from the village market to online marketplaces, it pretty much stays the same—you gather information about the person you're trading with, be it their eBay seller rating or customer comments or even just their Facebook page, and you make an intuitive decision about rates and terms. It's the same exact type of trade, except now the marketplace is global, so you have a larger pool of people with whom to make exchanges, and (often) more information to make the decision by. It's more people and more data, but it's certainly not a cognitive challenge to understand as a mechanism of exchange.

What was unanticipated is that along the way it increasingly makes geopolitical boundaries irrelevant. When I can trade with anyone, anywhere, at a price that's established by market forces and not political regulation, using currencies that are evaluated by demand instead of government fiat, then all of a sudden said regulation and government doesn't have much of a role to play in the exchange anymore.

In the days of the Wild West, banks weren't trusted because people feared the bankers would literally take their money and just leave. It took the Fed (Federal Reserve) guaranteeing that they'd cover the money for people to decide banks were OK. Now, with online reputation, there's nowhere to run anymore—your online identity persists whether you want it to or not, meaning that we don't need the Fed's guarantee as long as we trust that the exchange is worth less than the identity of the person we're trading with. That's true an increasing majority of the time, and as a result, online exchange is set to break the bank.

GIFT ECONOMIES AND OTHER EXAMPLES OF
REPUTATION EXCHANGE

To understand why modern banking's business model is so threatened by the availability of online reputation, we need to know how the bank (and financial regulation in general) came about in the first place, as well as the role reputation played in the systems that predicated it.

For most of human history we've used a variety of systems to regulate and assist in the exchange of goods and services. In the small village scenario, it was often direct trade, or barter, where you knew that a bushel of my corn was worth approximately one of your pigs. Mind you, that trade was then adjusted by whether we were good friends, if you'd helped my sister last winter, if you had heard good things about my corn this season, if we were aligned on village politics, et cetera. It's not necessarily simple, but barter *is* enormously intuitive: It relies directly on reputation. It's also the oldest method of exchange known to mankind, and our brains have had thousands of years of adaptation to evolve to it.

This same method of valuation—reputation—allows a multitude of other exchange systems, most of which are nonquantifiable. The idea of a single method of exchange is completely new—there is no evidence that societies relied on barter alone before using money for trade. Instead, most of the time nonmonetary societies used the principles of gift economics and debt. When barter did happen, it was usually between strangers. Rather than universally relying on a single, centralized system, people used the right kind of exchange method for each situation, the method that was most agreeable to both parties.

Gift economies are an interesting example, being a method of exchange quite different from market or commodity exchange such as barter. The idea is that voluntary and recurring gift exchanges both create and circulate wealth and consumption of goods while simultaneously building a community. As opposed to a market economy, informal customs (i.e., *culture*) govern gift economies rather than negotiated pricing, meaning that in order to function, everyone involved needs to understand and subscribe to the culture in question.

Most notably for this book, gift economies are based on the belief that goods are more valuable when shared, as opposed to through the exacerbation of value through scarcity. (Keep this point in mind—that scarcity and abundance-based economies are different—for later.) More specifically, even when goods are scarce, they're invested into a community in such a way that everyone benefits from their presence, not just those who receive them in a one-time trade.

At the same time, gift economies are designed to perpetuate themselves so that value doesn't disappear from the community in which they're invested. In his book *Debt: The First 5,000 Years*, anthropologist David Graeber describes the Tiv of West Africa, who believe that completing an economic transaction is immoral at its core, or at the very least rude, because it indicates that one party doesn't want to engage with the other in the future.[1] In other words, if a Tiv gives you a gift, you're supposed to respond with a gift of greater or lesser value. The difference, or debt, between you indicates that your relationship will continue. If you responded with a gift of equal value, you'd be implying that you wanted to end the relationship. It's an extension of the same idea: Gift economies work well in many cases because they tie people together through cultural bonds, providing value to both the community and individuals in ways that aren't strictly financial.

In modern times we see extensions of the gift economy idea manifesting in many ways, from the ideals behind donating food or even organs, to festivals like Burning Man, to those stacks of "free books" one finds in airports. The concept of giving freely with an expectation of having the favor later returned is deeply engrained in most cultures, whether you call it goodwill, good karma, or good sense.

Gift economy societies were usually small as well as geographically remote from each other, which makes sense—I don't want to engage in a gift exchange with someone who's going to up stakes and disappear over the hill right after I give them something big. As with barter, gift economies had the disadvantage of requiring that participants or their intermediaries physically meet face to face and that transactions be completed in a single swap. As a result, market exchange usually became dominant as political entities formed to regulate trade and commerce within their boundaries. (Again, for later in the book, keep in mind that there is no longer an "over the hill" to disappear to anymore; we're all networked ubiquitously now, wherever we might be.)

As precious metals such as gold and silver were introduced as currency, indirect trades separated by time and space became possible. As cities, states, and empires were established, more compact forms of specie like coins and contracts were minted or printed as fiat money with preset values, allowing asset accumulation that didn't dissolve over time the way a bushel of grain or a pig might. Critically, these new fiat currencies usually had the backing of a government or other body of law that could stabilize the value of the currency by producing more or less of it—or could go to war with someone who wanted to deflate the sources of value behind it.

AN ESCAPE FROM CENTRALIZED CONTROL

This government backing also helped solve price discovery. Price discovery is exactly what it sounds like. How do you know what your wool is worth on an open market, anyway? What's a fair price for chickens when I'm the only chicken farmer I know, but you say you have three others willing to sell to you in some other valley I've never been to?

"If we look way back we had hunting and gathering and barter as the price discovery mechanism," says Don Tapscott, a specialist in business strategy and author of *Wikinomics*, *Growing Up Digital*, and several other books. "Then the world was comprised of slave empires, and the price discovery mechanism was the slave auction, and then under feudalism the nobility established the price of most things."[2]

All of which is convenient if you don't happen to be a slave and also happen to be nobility, but it may not be the most equitable pricing strategy otherwise.

By way of illustration, Tapscott told me a story about a cardinal and a painting.

Some years ago Tapscott was in Rome where a cardinal's mansion had been renovated and turned into a museum. He had some spare time and took a guided tour, looking at a number of the paintings. At one point the guide stopped and pointed out a particular painting, saying, "This is interesting; the artist was Bernini. When he had created the painting the cardinal visited and told him, 'I like this painting and want to buy it.' Bernini said, 'It's not for sale,' to which the cardinal said, 'OK, then in that case I'll appropriate it and you can go to jail.' "

At this point Tapscott laughed, adding, "Now that's some highly leveraged price discovery." His point is that when you don't have access to information about other markets, you're very vulnerable to people who can set the price for you, because you don't know what leverage they might have over you. But it's still better than not being able to trade at all, which is a big part of why government backing and control over markets was so useful for such a long time.

MONEY SPRINGS FROM LOGISTICAL RESTRICTIONS

So we have some ideas of how trade happened before money became widespread. But how and why did money become so de facto? From Wikipedia:

> In historic times, the introduction of currency as a standardized money facilitated a wider exchange of goods and services. The circulation of a standardized currency provides the method of overcoming the major disadvantage to commerce through use of a barter system, the "double coincidence of wants" necessary for barter trades to occur. For example, if a man who makes pots for a living needs a new house, he may wish to hire someone to build it for him. But he cannot make an equivalent number of pots to equal this service done for him, because even if the builder could build the house, the builder might not want the pots. Currency solved this problem by allowing a society as a whole to assign values and thus to collect goods and services

effectively and to store them for later use, or to split them among several providers.

Today commerce includes a complex system of commercial entities that try to maximize their profits by offering products and services to the market (which consists both of individuals and other companies) at the lowest production cost. A system of international trade has helped to develop the world economy but, in combination with bilateral or multilateral agreements to lower tariffs or to achieve free trade, has sometimes harmed third-world markets for local products.[3]

In other words, the reason for the rise in dominance of representational, quantifiable currencies such as money was basically logistical restrictions. Money got around problems like finding the person who wanted to buy your product and then getting payments to you in a safe way. That's one popular theory, anyway. One competing theory suggests that credit and coins came as a result of serfs and soldiers being paid in methods that kept them beholden to their governments or owners. After all, if you can only spend your money at the army base, the army is going to have a pretty good handle on your liberty. Another theory states that barter didn't exist until you reached more advanced social systems, and instead what was most common were credit systems. Those credit systems were primarily restricted by a lack of means of distribution.

Either way, as commerce expanded due to improvements in travel and trade, the requirements on commerce only grew in complexity, to which money was increasingly the answer. During the twentieth century, fixed currencies (where the currency's value is fixed to another measure of value, such as gold) were gradually replaced by floating currencies (where a currency's value is allowed to fluctuate according to the foreign exchange market).

To give you an idea of the complexities engendered by floating currencies, take the dollar. When Richard Nixon abolished the gold standard in 1971, the US dollar became a true fiat currency, in which its value was only as good as the US government's word. This meant the Fed could print as much or as little of the currency as it liked. Now a true floating currency, the dollar became vulnerable, as conservative columnist David Frum liked to say, "to chronic inflation punctuated by bubbles."[4] Anyone who's paid attention to the US economy over the last 30 years could reasonably say Frum was onto something. The point here is that floating currencies are more manipulable by regulators, which is both a good and an evil; most importantly, they are more complex than simply pegging the dollar to gold.

Add to that complexity recent developments in computer networks that have made electronic transactions possible, resulting in financial exchanges that have rapidly increased in speed and complexity. Now we see transaction mechanisms ranging from straight purchases (where an item, good, or service is exchanged for money), to debit cards (which is a combination of a purchase and a loan), to derivatives (which are valued by reference to the values of other investments—and which took down Lehman Brothers and destabilized the entire US economy).

Note, by the way, that these destabilizing effects are no longer limited to one particular market or geopolitical entity. The world has become far too interconnected to avoid these entanglements. As a result, the US trading in derivatives led to worldwide repercussions, including, for example, the collapse of the entire financial economy in at least one country (Iceland) and widespread financial chaos in several others (such as Greece).

This is just the tip of the iceberg when it comes to modern financial complexity. As we've seen in the recent collapses in both the United States and Europe, this complexity does not necessarily lend itself to reliability. Nevertheless, financial economics has become the global standard for commerce for hundreds of years because it can do what gift and barter economies could not—it could scale.

That scale makes a huge difference. Representational currencies like dollars and cents work well because I can take a bundle of them to a total stranger on your behalf and buy goods and services with them. That kind of trade is hard to do when your only alternative is to live in the same village as said stranger. Up until now gift economies and barter only operated well with people you knew, and most of the time that meant the people who lived nearby.

All that changed with the arrival of the Internet. Suddenly, all these alternative systems of exchange—many of which are much more intuitive, more beneficial to the group, or use different methods of valuation—are viable beyond the tiny geographically restricted groups they were available to before. That opens up some significant new markets across the globe.

SYSTEM D—THE "OTHER" GLOBAL COMMERCE MARKET

In the West we like to think that our financial system has worked very well. For the few of us who live in the top global economic bracket, it certainly has. But that leaves a pretty big segment of the human race out of the equation, and it turns out they're not just sitting around waiting for the situation to change. The concepts behind reputation economics—trust, multiple currencies for exchange, the use of barter, trade, and gifts, et cetera—are all already in play in the second-biggest economy on the planet. The only reason you haven't heard about it yet is that it's almost entirely illegal.

I'm talking about the black market. The Organization for Economic Co-Operation and Development (OECD) concluded in 2009 that half the world's workers (almost 1.8 billion people) were employed not by the traditional economy, but some kind of "shadow economy." The OECD predicts that by 2020, this shadow economy will employ two-thirds of the entire planet's workers.[5]

In an article for *Foreign Policy*, Robert Neuwirth explains:

> System D is a slang phrase pirated from French-speaking Africa and the Caribbean. The French have a word that they often use to describe particularly effective and motivated people. They call them *débrouillards*. To say a man is a débrouillard is to tell people how resourceful and ingenious he is. The former French colonies have sculpted this word to their own social and economic reality. They say that inventive, self-starting, entrepreneurial merchants who are doing business on their own, without registering or being regulated by the bureaucracy and, for the most part, without paying taxes, are part of *l'economie de la débrouillardise*.

Or, put in street terms (which are almost always sexier than what economists come up with), "*Systeme D.*"[6]

It's not limited to particular locations, either. According to one *Bloomberg Businessweek* report, "In more than 50 countries around the world, the shadow economy is at least 40 percent the size of documented GDP."[7] In other words, every country has at least two economies: one official and regulated, and a shadowy one that is almost half the size of the total value of the country that is self- or unregulated. Critically, that shadow economy, unlike most regulated economies, is growing.

It was also there first. Keep in mind, in the absence of centralized authorities, most markets are unregulated and end up relying on the same methods of social control that are central to all our modern social software and exchange platforms: reputation. All of which means that we're essentially seeing the original market—some derivative or other of which human beings have used for our entire existence—enjoying a resurgence in the face of a rapidly eroding global financial system which is in many ways failing to meet our needs.

It's exciting to think about; a completely unregulated marketplace quickly replacing the global banking system with networks of trust? A global meritocracy in the making that will create a truly balanced market of self-motivated participants? What could be better?

But the black market has its downsides, too. There's a reason slavery, heroin, and child pornography tend to be found in illegal markets—there's some serious social costs for supporting them commercially. A completely open market is open completely, and unless the marketplace cares enough to act on restricting those goods there's nothing to keep suppliers from growing at least as large as demand exists for their products.

THE ORIGINAL BANKLESS BANKING SYSTEM

Which brings us back to the question at hand. Is money the only answer to scaleable commerce? Or, more specifically, is centralized fiat currency really required to facilitate general trade? To answer that, let me introduce you to *hawala*, which in Arabic means "transfer." Hawala is also called *hundi* and "is an informal value transfer system based on the performance and honor of a huge network of money brokers, which are primarily located in the Middle East, North Africa, the Horn of Africa, and the Indian subcontinent. It is basically a parallel or alternative remittance system that exists or operates outside of, or parallel to traditional banking or financial channels."[8]

Hawala is *old*. It has origins in classical Islamic law and is mentioned in Islamic jurisprudence texts as early as the eighth century. It's believed to have originally arisen for financing long-distance trade between emerging capital trade centers in the early medieval period. In South Asia, it was only gradually replaced by a formal banking system in the first half of the twentieth century.

Hawala is very simple. In the most basic variant of the system, money is transferred through a network of *hawaladars*, or hawala brokers, who transfer the money without actually moving it. It works like this:

Let's say I want to send $100 to my mother in Chile. I approach a hawaladar and give him a password and $100. I know this guy, and so does my family, my coworkers, and other folks in my town, so he already has a decent idea who my mother is. Then I send my mom the password. The hawaladar contacts a hawaladar he knows who contacts a hawaladar who knows a hawaladar in my mom's hometown. My mom goes to this guy and tells him the password, and he gives her $100. Later, the hawaladars settle the debt among themselves using whatever currency or value exchange they want.

That's it. No promissory instruments. No contracts. No legal enforceability of claims requiring a legal or even juridical environment. Instead, it relies on trust and the extensive use of connections, such as regional affiliations or family relationships. Even more importantly, the hawaladars don't have to get paid in any particular currency, or even currency at all. They can trade goats, real estate, employees, time, or anything else they mutually agree on.

It's easy to write this off as a cute cultural artifact. But hawala is amazingly robust and has what geeks call "strong error detection" built in—a feature that makes hawala superior to our existing banking system in many ways. As an example, take the Mumbai attackers of 2008. They used this off-the-grid, personal trust system to transfer all their funds. Investigators in India knew this, and quickly used the hawala network to penetrate deep into the terrorist network. This helped authorities dismantle a systemic flow of money that had its origins in the powerful and legendarily secretive intelligence services of Pakistan.

Say what? What happened here?

In the case of the terrorists behind the 9/11 attack, an institution-based system stymied human investigators because those institutions had little to gain from transparency and personal trust. They only had to fulfill the letter of the law (US government banking regulations), which they had long ago figured out how to game and therefore had no stake in improving. In the case in Mumbai, investigators met personally with people—those who made every last part of the hawala network—who traded first and foremost on their reputations and did not want to see that sullied by an association with terrorists.

While the funders and attackers were radical jihadists bent on killing innocents, the intermediaries they used were common hawala brokers who make nearly all of their money moving funds as loans for small businesses, expatriates helping their families back home to pay bills, et cetera. They are not involved in drug-running, prostitution, and *especially* not terrorism. These intermediaries would have suffered severe reputation damage and thus lost their primary source of income if their name became associated with violent killers of innocent people. The Indian investigators knew this, exploited it, and inflicted a serious blow to terror operations in their country for years to come.

Sometimes, who you know can make all the difference—and hawala doesn't work without knowing people.

HOW THE INTERNET WORKS (ROUGHLY)

Let me take a moment here to explain how the Internet works. Don't worry, it'll be relatively painless (as well as impossibly general—but hopefully useful for this point). As originally invented by Sir Tim Berners-Lee, the Internet runs on data that is chopped up into packets. Each server (or computer connected to the Internet) takes these packets and passes them to the next server that is likely to be closer to the end destination than the others that are nearby. That server does the same, and eventually the packets all find their way to the destination server, which puts them back together again in a useful way, and—voila!—you get your eBay page. Or your e-mail. Or your Facebook timeline.

Now obviously there are some security concerns here, so sometimes the packets are split up using encryption. That is, a password of a sort is used to verify that any particular set of packets hasn't been tampered with. In this case the transmission process works exactly the same, except that at the end of all these packets being passed around, the password is used to validate that all the right data has arrived at the destination server without being altered.

Sound familiar? This is exactly how hawala works. And just like hawala, the Internet has been so world-changing not in small part due to its openness—the willingness of all the servers along the way to pass packets along. This trust relationship has enabled the circumvention of government suppression (such as during the Arab Spring), the defeat of widespread censorship, and free growth of massively connected networks like Facebook and Twitter and LinkedIn, among a million other wonderful things. And keep in mind, hawala occurred well before traditional banking was even a glimmer in some money-lender's eye. It's worked for (literally) thousands of years. And what's more, it's not only functioning well today, it's *thriving*.

ERASING LOGISTICAL RESTRICTIONS

That's where the world has changed. A few short decades ago a technological innovation appeared that allowed you to establish a relationship with someone you *didn't* live in the same village with, someone with whom you may only have had a shared interest. Suddenly it was possible to communicate regularly—often in real time—with otherwise complete strangers, and to establish very real relationships with them. For the first time, you could share reputation with anyone, anywhere on the globe.

This strange new frontier, the Internet, was at first only the domain of academics and scientists. But it proved to be enormously effective in all the ways that gift economies and barter systems always had been. What's more, it was effective between people who could never have otherwise exchanged information, culture, insight, or goods or services. As the technology supporting these communications evolved from text-only chat forums to voice-over-IP phone calls to high-resolution video conferencing, gift economies and barter systems were freed of the constraints that had previously prevented them from competing with financial currencies; namely, you could now trade with people you knew, *anywhere.*

The expansion of the Internet has continued to give rise to this resurgence of the reputation economy, most particularly in the technology sector, where those selfsame communication technologies first got their start. Open-source projects are created and shared by scientists, engineers, and software developers. The Linux operating system is a prototypical example of the gift economy's prominence in the technology sector and its active role in instating the use of permissive software licenses that allow free reuse and sharing of software and knowledge.

Science is another prominent example that has been described as a gift economy, as is academia, both of which often require peer review (i.e., free sharing) as part of the valuation process. Note also that academia often reimburses its participants in tenure and promotion, but not necessarily in financial remuneration: The currency here is reputation. Increasingly, barter and gift economies are becoming the norm of exchange in widespread social software platforms, from Yelp to eBay to Facebook.

For the first time since market economies took precedence, the tables may be turning on what we often call *finance* (monetary exchange) when what we mean is *commerce* (the exchange of goods and services). The important point here is in the scale along which these systems evolved. If you take a foot-long ruler, divided into 12 inches, and match it to the extent of human history, you could plot the presence of barter, trade, and gift economies along the first 11.75 inches—it's the primary form of commerce human brains evolved to use. That last quarter inch is financial commerce, which, to a startling majority of us, often seems painfully unintuitive.

Given that, quantifiable and fiat currency commerce starts to look like a flash in the pan. As we'll see, it's a commerce system that may be on the way out. That's because at the same time technologies are optimizing our intuitive methods of commerce to a newly globalized world, we're beginning to develop new means of exchange that actually *create more value* for the people who use them. It's a condition that sounds as implausible as a perpetual motion machine.

But it's not.

CHAPTER 3
THE FRACTIONATION OF CURRENCY

WHY COMMERCE AS IT EXISTS NOW IS BROKEN, AND WAYS REPUTATION REPLACES IT

A big part of the appeal of black market and new-technology methods of exchange is that they're circumventing regulations and limitations people don't want or need anymore. But even more importantly, reputation economics is able to account for all the elements of value in a transaction in a way that lets more people benefit from them.

Rather than just the dollar value of an exchange, we're now able to account for the ethical return on buying fair trade coffee, the emotional return on buying a handmade product, the relational return on doing a favor for a friend. These portions of value in an exchange were previously ethereal—inexplicable to the equation of the financial transaction. They were fractions of the exchange that were ignored, left on the table in any transaction in favor of the convenience pure finance offered. Not anymore.

That change means other benefits to any particular transaction are suddenly valid reasons to have the exchange in the first place. This prompts a whole wide variety of new types of commerce—and value analysis—that simply wouldn't have happened before, with the result that consumers are behaving in new and inexplicable ways.

INFINITE FRACTIONS OF VALUE

For most of the history of finance, limiting methods and means of exchange has been beneficial because it gave more control to the regulators of same. Remember, the big problem for most of human history has been how to meet the person who wanted to buy your products when you wanted to sell them. One of the side effects of being the middleman is that you can regulate the terms of the exchange, ensuring, for example, that the person selling the milk properly pasteurized it so the person who buys it doesn't get sick when they drink it.

But now we're suddenly able to not only meet that person, anywhere on the globe, but also to instantly know everything we need about them to confidently make an exchange with them— and to ensure social repercussions (at least) if they screw us over. This turns the benefits of heavily regulated commerce on its head, as said regulations often simply slow down the dynamics of market valuation and speed of exchange.

More importantly, the more methods of value exchange the better, because it means we can find more and more ways of extracting value through nonfungible markets. For example, a dollar can't buy me goodwill from my sister, but trading surplus wool with her knitting club certainly can. That goodwill might be worth more to me than the dollar value of the wool, and now, for the first time, I have the means to measure, store, and trade it. Value is relative, and the existence of globally available and persistent reputation platforms means I can find the best market for both my goods and my valuations. I'm no longer restricted to a single market's exchange rate—I can now pick from millions, all based on my personal model of value.

That fact alone—the existence of infinite markets within which to maximize the value of an exchange *for our own personal definition of value*—changes everything. All the rest is effectively window dressing, albeit window dressing which supports the existing global financial system. As a side effect, exchange starts to be mediated more by reputation than regulation, and gift economies become more efficient in many cases than financial exchange, because they operate as an abundance economy and generate more value for everyone involved in the trade.

EXPERIENCES, NOT THINGS

What's interesting about all these new tools and methods of exchange, particularly now that they're based on escalating and increasingly powerful platforms and technologies, is that they're landing in the midst of a major shift in cultural perspectives around what commerce is in the first place.

The big economic platforms of the day—the dollar, euro, and yen—are each individually as shaky as they've ever been, and between the housing market bubble in the United States and the debt crisis in Europe, the possibility of large-scale financial collapse has never seemed more real. Closer to home, consider that the United States has its greatest level of debt, *ever*, at roughly $17 trillion. College debt rates are nearing $30,000 a student, nearly one in five households have student loans,[1] and overall unemployment is at its highest since 1965.[2]

With all this bad news right outside the door, you'd expect people to either be stuffing their dollars under a mattress or drowning their woes in a bottle. Instead, we're seeing something unusual. People are spending more than ever—they're just not spending it on stuff, and they're often not doing it with money.

"There's a big shift from people buying material goods to people buying experiences," says Anya Kamenetz, a longtime millennials researcher and author of *Generation Debt*, *DIY U*, and an upcoming book on the future of tests. "It's filtering into the mass consciousness that experience is worth more in the long run than the latest shiny new object."[3]

What's more, Kamenetz suggests there's more value to an experience than what dollars can buy directly. "Reputation exchanges tend more towards the experiential side because there's a relationship involved," says Kamenetz. "For example, I may rent my apartment out on Airbnb ostensibly so someone will take care of my cat, but really I may be motivated to meet people with whom I have a structured, trusted relationship."

In this way reputation exchanges are used by platforms such as Airbnb, Skillshare, or even eBay to allow users to get more with their dollars. They're investing time to establish a reputation, and in turn they're able to garnish—or replace—their purchases with experiences. In the typical view of commerce you can't buy "meeting an interesting and unexpected person to take care of my cat" in any useful (or generally platonic) way, but through Airbnb you can definitely improve your chances. The result is that people are starting to trade on more than just the numeric evaluation of physical goods and are instead spending on experiences that their networks have allowed them to trade nonfinancial valuables to enhance.

Kamenetz puts it this way: "Given that experiential goods have much more value the more we're invested in them relationally, they're definitively encroaching on strictly financial exchanges. There's a self realization aspect to these purchases that you simply can't get with dollars."

It's hard to compete with self-realization once you've got the first few levels of Maslow's hierarchy of needs covered—after food, shelter, and safety, people are starting to prioritize experiences that enrich their lives and ideas of who they are. Increasingly, it seems like people are realizing that it doesn't take a new car and a penthouse apartment to do that.

TIME VS. MONEY: THE END OF WORKING FOR PAY ALONE

This all sounds very nice—the First World has so overcome problems of satisfying its citizens' basic needs that we're now all embarking on quests of self-realization. Except I don't believe that. Again, what about that staggering national debt, the collapse of the education system, and rising unemployment? To get a reality check I turned to Marina Gorbis, the head of the Institute for the Future (IFTF). The IFTF has been in the business of prognostication and analysis of real-world trends since 1968, and it's not because they're bad at it.

"It's true, younger people don't have as many jobs available, and they're increasingly having a very jaded view of work for pay. They saw their parents get jettisoned from jobs they hated, and have vowed to work at jobs that offer more fulfilling returns than a paycheck," says Gorbis. "They view their time differently and recognize that it is a valuable commodity. Not many of them will be willing to sell their time for pay alone."[4]

In a very real way, it appears the declining job market, lack of opportunity, and increasing pressure to squeeze more value out of every dollar are driving people *away* from traditional methods of exchange. Being able to get more return from investing in a trip to Italy—even if it means having to skip that latte once a week, or putting off buying a car yet another year—becomes a priority when you can't have both. And when you can't have both—or even that new iPhone or hot new Prada jacket—then having a meaningful experience is a hell of a good alternative.

ACCESS, NOT OWNERSHIP

The rise of the experiential marketplace isn't happening due to financial pressures alone. A lot of it has to do with the proliferation of *access* that people now have thanks to our widespread social platforms. Skillshare lets us earn a little extra income practicing skills we couldn't monetize otherwise. TaskRabbit lets us get tasks done conveniently and on our own terms. Etsy lets us buy from craftspeople whose stories we relate to, Kickstarter to invest in projects we believe in. All at a price and under conditions that are personalized for us alone.

Sunny Bates is on the board of Kickstarter and has been instrumental in guiding enterprises from TED (conferences) to Creative Capital (investors) to General Electric and the Standard. When it comes to identifying major shifts in consumer behavior and emerging investment trends, they don't get much better. She put it best when she told me, "It's about access, not ownership."[5]

A lot of the ability to share so readily has to do with urbanization and the centralization of resources. For example, Bates's daughter is doing lots of work interviewing millennials. Apparently, many of them feel like failures because they live with other people or at home.

But it's their response to this impetus that gets interesting. Because urbanization has brought together all the requirements for modern living in one place, people are better able to enjoy the free aspects of culture. It's cheaper to go to a park than a club, and easier to flashmob a party at a friend's place than pay for a private concert. "There are other measures of success than 'being rich,'" says Bates. "The reality is that when they stop to think about it, people aren't interested in living in a mansion with a coke habit and a bunch of hookers. They're interested in sharing their successes—and sharing is the operative word. The question isn't how to make the most money anymore, it's how do we create stuff where people feel free about how they're living and working?"

In this way, access is simply worth more than the available possible ownership. As Kamenetz says, "Millennials have a very different view; they have low earnings, lots of debt, and less opportunities overall. But they're not upset about it—they're more optimistic than you'd expect. Part of that is because they are very high in reputation value in their lives. They use networks to compensate for their lack of material goods.

"It can be as simple as 'I'm less employed, but have more time. I don't have money to buy a bottle at the club, but I know the DJ over here who can let me in for free.' "

The emphasis on experience, and living life on your own terms, is reflected in how people are choosing their work. One example is BrainPickings.org. Maria Popova, author of the popular blog, professes to love her world and her life *without* advertisers. Since BrainPickings first launched in 2006, it has earned millions of page views and generated side gigs for Popova as a culture writer for *The Atlantic*, *Wired UK*, *GOOD*, and *Nieman Labs*. But Popova refuses to take advertising. Why? Because it would force her to write to satisfy the advertisers, to co-opt her work to maximize her page views instead of focusing on the content she believes in. And it works: Based on donations alone Popova is able to enjoy work and a lifestyle she seems very happy with.

As Bates put it, "In the idea of reputation economics we take obsolete or outmoded ideas about success and what that looks like and put them on top of very different ways of earning and thinking about our money." Bates would know; she's been forging her own path as a superconnector for years, including consulting, talent acquisition, startup consulting, and more. It was never the "normal" 9 to 5, and as a result she, like Popova, has developed a lifestyle that suits her particular strengths and interests.

The way millennials look for the work they do also reflects this. "They'll find possibilities through people they know and not what they look like on paper. For young people today job security means nothing because they're always looking around for something better," says Bates. "They don't believe in loyalty after a full lifetime of layoffs and they know that 'job security,' isn't. For them, loyalty is a sacrifice, an opportunity cost, when the job isn't keeping their end of the bargain."

COLLABORATIVE CONSUMPTION: SHARING VS. OWNING

One of the best examples of this mentality of access is in collaborative consumption, or the sharing of resources. Car sharing is a premier example of this; on any of a number of platforms (RelayRides, CarSharing.us, or Car2go are all good examples), anyone can list their car for rent to anyone nearby for whatever time or rates they choose when they're not using it themselves. But there are many others: Neighborgoods, for instance, which allows you to loan or rent anything you own (such as garden shears, a ladder, or a blender) to anyone else nearby. Or Skillshare, which lets you teach classes on anything you happen to know a great deal about. The list goes on and on.

All these instances are examples of reputation systems allowing individuals to connect to others who want what they have and to earn the trust of additional others by demonstrating their value. And these systems are working; beyond the majority of people for whom these are secondary income streams on the side—incidental gigs or rentals or what have you—there are a growing number for whom these new means of production are becoming their primary career.

Programmer Avi Flombaum quit his job as CTO at a startup because his hobby teaching Skillshare classes earned him $100,000. He earned that in one year—more than most teachers make in traditional schools. The same model also works broadly rather than deeply, as in the case of the First Annual Whatcom Skillshare Faire, a community event where nearly 600 people took and gave hour-long classes in everything from beekeeping to basic carpentry to how to start a small business. In both cases, otherwise employed (or underemployed) people took resources which were underutilized by themselves and offered them to others using online trust platforms.

This trend is on the rise for many reasons. The first of those is that people need it. In our current economy, many are having difficulty finding full-time work and therefore need to pinch every penny. Additionally, it's more efficient, boosting productivity by making resources available that would otherwise not be attainable, lowering barriers to entrepreneurship through same, and helping facilitate markets even when cash is hard to come by. Finally, it's growing because we've got web platforms that match buyers and sellers, promote trust and validate reputations, and facilitate exchanges.[6]

There are problems, of course. Early on in Airbnb's history, one homeowner came back to discover that her renters had gone on a meth-fueled binge in which they stole all her grandmother's jewelry, ransacked her house (including lighting things on fire), and gutted her walls to search for valuables. Airbnb has since established a $1,000,000 guarantee—their faith in their reputation system is so strong (and with their massive growth curve they have a right to be) that they'll pay that much to cover any damages any guest may make.[7]

SELF VS. CENTRALIZED REGULATION

Airbnb's million-dollar guarantee is an interesting case of self-regulation, or of market-enforced regulation in which reputation acts as the driving factor. Instead of legislation enforcing regulation—which is what is typically done for things like drug use or gun safety—Airbnb recognized very clearly that what made them money was the trust in their reputation system, and that such trust was worth $1,000,000.

It's an important example of how, by participating in the eco-system of users and expectations, a company can find a natural set point of value versus service. A million dollars may seem like a huge investment, but it's likely Airbnb pays it out very infrequently, and the confidence it instills in the system more than offsets the cost.

The point here is that a company can fix a reputation by responding openly and responsibly to their community, an act that drives increased adoption due to the confidence such acts inspire in existing users. That sort of self-responsibility just isn't common with today's corporate entities, who tend to respond by cleaving to the letter of the law with regulations and by using broad-stroke media campaigns to cover up problems rather than make expensive investments in their communities.

If self-regulation works well for some organizations, it's still not a good enough answer for many. The idea that these businesses will create an informal economy without the safety nets of social security, health insurance, anti-discrimination, and taxation is anarchic for a lot of people used to the legislation-enforced method of business assurance we've grown used to over the last century. With good reason—we've all seen organizations that aren't regulated act outside the interests of the general public. The environmental impact of big industries like petrochemical or mining in the first half of this century are pretty good examples.

But those examples are thoroughly grounded in the context of their times. Legislation and regulation as exercised today are primarily artifacts of highly centralized, authority-restricted hierarchies such as government. Which isn't to say they can't work well; just that they typically work slowly, are expensive, and tend toward centralized power.

That runs absolutely counter to how emerging businesses like Skillshare or Airbnb are developing—and responding—quickly to the needs and expectations of their users. In cases like these user confidence, or their reputation, is critical to maintain and quick to evaporate. If Airbnb had launched a cover-up campaign of radio ads and magazine articles to lead users away from the story of the meth addict attack, it would just have solidified users' expectation that the company refused to take responsibility. The more they tried to cover it up, the more users would have focused on the story (the dreaded "Barbara Streisand Effect"), and the less chances Airbnb would have had to recover potential customers to their service.

Instead they did the right thing, admitted the problem, and "did right" by the expectations of the users. And they did it in days or weeks, not the months or years it would have taken big government to decide how to act and legislate appropriately.

Car service Uber is a sterling example of this approach, embodied in a white paper they released in early 2013. Uber takes any call (or lets you use a convenient smartphone app) to request a car to a specific location. An available driver accepts your request, and you get a text message telling you a car is on its way along with its estimated arrival time. You get in, the driver already knows where to take you thanks to the app, and once you arrive your fare is automatically deducted from your credit card—tip included. All you need is an Uber account and a working cell phone.

Where this gets interesting is when Uber reversed its decision not to provide its services in a number of markets due to the regulations there. From their white paper:

> Over the last year, new startups have sought to compete with Uber by offering transportation services without traditional commercial insurance or licensing. Uber refrained from participating in this technology sector—known as ridesharing—due to regulatory risk that ridesharing drivers may be subject to

fines or criminal misdemeanors for participating in non-licensed transportation for compensation.

In most cities across the country, regulators have chosen not to enforce against non-licensed transportation providers using ridesharing apps. This course of non-action resulted in massive regulatory ambiguity leading to one-sided competition which Uber has not engaged in to its own disadvantage. It is this ambiguity which we are looking to address with Uber's new policy on ridesharing:

1. Uber will roll out ridesharing on its existing platform in any market where the regulators have given tacit approval;

2. In the absence of regulatory leadership, Uber will implement safeguards in terms of safety and insurance that will go above and beyond what local regulatory bodies have in place for commercial transportation.

In the face of this challenge, Uber could have chosen to do nothing. We could have chosen to use regulation to thwart our competitors. Instead, we chose the path that reflects our company's core: we chose to compete.[8]

One could well argue that this was the only sensible path open to Uber because they've no fans among regulators and wouldn't have been able to succeed in taking that route—Uber has famously flouted regulatory efforts in cities like San Francisco and New York City in the past. On the other hand, their response makes a lot of sense; they've essentially said they'll roll out ridesharing where it's not forbidden and will do a better job at self-regulating than their competitors. As long as they do a good enough job that it satisfies consumers, that may well be enough—and will certainly be more than what regulators would be able to legislate in the time it takes for consumers to come to expect the service.

Another aspect to this element of self-regulation is that many of these innovations are emerging out of markets that are under-served.

San Francisco famously has bad taxi service for a variety of reasons, the most salient of which are:

a) Because of the bureaucratic structure of cab licensing in San Francisco, cab companies make money renting cabs to drivers and don't care if the consumer is happy with the service or not. As a result, there is little motivation to improve their services by creating, say, a centralized dispatch system. This means you're limited to calling a single company at a time until you get through.

b) Labor law states that if a cab company farms out its cars to independent contractors, it doesn't have to pay expensive disability and social security taxes, and that the contractor drivers can't unionize (and so have little power to change the working agreement). The arrangement seems to be working for the cab companies: The United Taxicab Workers (UTW), a coalition working to improve driver conditions, released confidential financial statements from one of San Francisco's largest cab firms and found that the company earned a 50 percent profit in gross revenues of nearly $19 million. By way of comparison, a full-time driver makes an average of $20,000 to $30,000 a year.

c) Conversely, there's no law that says drivers have to pick up a call. As a result, many stick to fares who flag them down in the street, look likely to tip big, or are headed in a direction they want to go. Again, the circumstances of regulation, law, and incumbent businesses create an environment where consumer interests play no role in what makes for a profitable job for the drivers.

Because of all this there was a dire need for more cabs in San Francisco, a need which Uber met by leveraging online platforms and technological scale to effectively automate the distribution of needed rides to available drivers—and matched it with a reputation platform in which you could rate drivers to ensure that a meritocracy of capable drivers rose to the top.

Is it perfect? No, of course not, and it is yet to be seen if a case of murder or theft mars the service's reputation or prompts it to put in place further guarantees. But the example is salient to the concept of reputation economics because it's a circumstance that's seen the world over: There is a solution or service needed that the financial economy, existing government, or incumbent business entities are not addressing, and a reputation system is able to supersede it. (Note that this same circumstance exists around censorship and human rights, but more on that later.)

Despite this prevalence of existing need and potential supply, regulators continue to demand legislative countermeasures while services continue to pop up that effectively ignore—or profit despite—them. Craigslist is still a buy-at-your-own-risk platform. Ridesharing services like Uber continue to thrive, despite ongoing legal hurdles. (The California Public Utilities Commission sent a cease-and-desist warning to both Lyft and SideCar, two other ridesharing services in San Francisco, and yet both are still growing.)

Why? Because there is a significant market for it. Collaborative consumption isn't likely to go away just because some people feel it's not regulated enough; the reputation systems they're built on are already proving adequate to sustain ongoing growth. A few meth-fueled home destructions are only causing the ecosystem to evolve—to the tune of million-dollar guarantees. That's a sign of a maturing industry, not a flash in the pan.

DONATING IS WORTH MORE THAN BUYING

Clay Shirky is a writer, consultant, and teacher on the social and economic effects of Internet technologies. While discussing reputation economics and what it meant for the future of commerce, he pointed out that consumers are increasingly making purchasing decisions based on intangible returns. For example, "The *New York Times* recently added a threshold charge; if you use the site over a certain amount they ask you to pay. What's interesting is that 75 to 80 percent of users never reach that point—most readers read one story, which they linked to from somewhere else."[9]

Of those 15 to 25 percent most don't pay but just leave instead. "That means that something like 3 percent of the entire *New York Times* audience are paying to support the site. What's interesting is that the *New York Times* thinks of this as a fee for service, but when you say 'Your deal is no different than NPR's' they get enraged."

NPR (National Public Radio) solicits donations once or twice a year; it bills itself as a public service and depends on a small percentage of its listeners to donate so it can continue to provide that service. The *New York Times*, on the other hand, thinks of itself as a commercial business, which depends on a small percentage of its readers to pay so it can continue.

The surprising caveat lies in the fact that the *New York Times* might be more successful if it recognized it has the same model as NPR and presented it as such. "The more you say it's just a commercial transaction the less people pay," says Shirky. "But if you say the *New York Times* might go out of business if you don't pay, people are much more likely to do so. If you present the commitment as being too commercial they're less willing; if you present it as preservation of a useful institution they're more willing."

The intimation is that people will *give* money for something they want to support, but are less inclined to *pay* for something they're charged for if they have the option. In other words, the intangible return of seeing your beliefs affirmed through the preservation of an institution you relate to is significantly more valuable than the financial worth of the good itself.

WHO'S DRIVING THIS BUS?

It's easy to infer from all this that somehow online or new-model services are more honest and more responsive than other forms of commerce. But the heads of these businesses are driven by many of the same motivations as the heads of big box companies—profit is still a big part of capitalism. The difference in many cases is that online services are exposed more regularly to the brutal efficiencies of an increasingly transparent marketplace.

Nobody's business is as vulnerable to being replaced by some kids in a garage as one that exists only virtually. Similarly, if your business relies on reputation-based networks of trust, you're going to think much more intuitively about the benefits of radical honesty to your customers.

That doesn't mean online companies are inherently more trustworthy, or that they don't or won't make the same harmful self-serving decisions a non-virtualized company would. It just means they're playing ball with the new rules every day, which makes it easier to anticipate alternatives that, as a side effect, can create more intangible returns for themselves and for their users. That edge is available to any company out there that recognizes that investing in new models and methods of engaging customers is key to survival in the new economy.

That research and development (R&D) is getting more and more important as these intangible returns become driving factors for consumers everywhere through their evolution into valid elements of every exchange. The result is that "consumer behavior" just isn't making much sense for a lot of preexisting systems. The new model of car is still sitting on the showroom floor, and nobody's screaming for the corner office. The old world order is getting turned on its head, and nobody seems to know why.

My opinion is that the answer lies with this sea change in how and what people are looking to exchange—in their use of reputation economies. Because as we shift from chasing after that next brass ring (or corner office, or new car, or younger wife) to focusing on our relationships, our self-satisfaction, or whatever else really matters to us, the old models of control suddenly fail.

It's similar to when the industrial revolution prompted a massive shift in where value was centralized, produced, and managed, toppling existing oligarchies and reshaping the face of the global economy. That was what the steam engine did—now we're dealing with the Internet, which effectively makes that engine available, simultaneously, to everybody. So what does that mean for existing markets and means of doing business today?

CHAPTER 4

THE RISE OF THE INDIVIDUAL

This shift in values—and concomitant behaviors—by consumers is causing huge problems for corporations. After all, consumers are (optimally) supposed to behave in predictable ways to allow for price maximization. When they suddenly start giving things away for free, or worse, not buying anything, it kind of throws a wrench in the system.

This change is happening in some significant ways. As an example, take car sales. Owning a car has been a sign of freedom, independence, and downright American Pride for much of the country's history. Ever since automobile lobbyists ruined the potential for a serious railway system, the United States has been synonymous with cars. Car parks, drive-in movies, the open road, multilane highways, the SUV, the Cadillac, drag racing, and more—throughout it all the US national identity and cars have been closely linked.

Except now they aren't anymore. In June of 2013 car sales saw an 18.8 percent decline. In fact, while we've recently seen a bump in car sales overall—the three years leading up to 2013 have shown significant improvement—2012 auto sales were still nearly 1.8 million below 2007, when sales were 16.2 million. US auto sales bottomed out in 2009, when GM and Chrysler declared bankruptcy. Sales that year were only 10.4 million, the lowest point for US auto sales per capita since World War II. 2009 sales were down nearly 3 million units from 2008, which was down almost 3 million units from 2007.

Part of that is due to the overall depression in the US economy of recent years, but even that can't account for the severity of the trend. It's even worse in Europe, where passenger car registrations were down by 10.2 percent in March (as published by the European manufacturers association ACEA). That's a decline for the eighteenth consecutive month.

So what happened? Consumer attitudes changed. People started realizing they didn't have to buy a new car every year. Having the latest model fresh off the lot stopped being equated with one's success in life—at least for a lot of us—at the same time more and more people started moving to cities. Once there, they didn't *need* those cars anymore, because public transit often existed and in any case needed resources were closer.

This rejection of established socio-commercial systems, like the idea that everyone needs to own their own car, is expanding. People are owning less "stuff" and investing in experiences, instead. This rejection is leading to a bevy of new systems eating the markets out from under dated methods of commerce and industry, and those industries that relied on them aren't very happy about it.

Unfortunately, the problem is only getting worse. Not only are people replacing outmoded systems, they're starting to actively fight against them. They can do this because of two main forces. The first is the motivating power of reputation—the increasing expectation that they can ask, and deserve to have answered, what the hell a company is really doing on their behalf. Combine that with the second, which is the enabling power of technology to find out what a company actually *is* doing and to join up with other people to punish it if it's unethical or damaging.

Normally that's the role of government. If so, things just got a whole lot more democratic. The real problem, though, is that a lot of those companies are doing things that people have every right to be unhappy about.

BAD COMPANY, NO CUSTOMERS

The obfuscation of information to manipulate markets, widespread use of tax havens, pernicious patent trolling, lobbyist and campaign "donations" used to enforce or create laws that favor expiring business models. We're all familiar with the ethically suspect schemes of the rich and famous—big corporations being first among them.

Part of the problem is that companies are treated as individuals, but are in fact *aggregations* of individuals. This means that each person in a company can hide their actions behind a larger entity that has the financial and legal means, as well as an utter lack of moral imperative, to avoid paying the price for its actions. If I'm working for a major financial firm and decide to sell subprime mortgages because it increases my year-end bonus, there's almost no disincentive to doing so. The worst that's likely to happen is that I'll get a lower bonus if we don't cash out appropriately. I don't need to think about the thousands of families who lose their homes, have their careers destroyed, or are forced to participate in a near-global recession—that's all a bit beyond my pay grade. And yet that exact same kind of decision caused exactly those repercussions in the big financial collapse in the United States earlier this century.

The result of this individually logical decision making is a mismatch between consumer expectation and corporate behavior. When I buy something from a seller on eBay I expect them to act decently, and if they don't I expect my negative review of them to have a serious impact. But when I buy a product from Best Buy they don't really give a damn if I'm not satisfied as long as I can't get too much of an audience to sympathize with my being upset. In fact, it's in their best interest to make it difficult for me to return a product, file a complaint, enlist the help of their customer support department, or otherwise cost them anything they can measure in dollars or cents because the less they do for me the less they have to spend. But this sort of attitude is becoming increasingly intolerable to consumers, who are beginning to expect the free and open sharing of information—and individual respect in exchange—they experience online.

Similarly, means of profit that used to be "normal" to organizations are becoming unacceptable to customers who are recognizing that the fees are no longer relevant. Like banks that require five to seven days to change a single value in one database entry (bank account) to another because back in the annals of time it took five to seven days to physically ship the gold that represented that value a certain distance, and the bank could take a percent by "owning" the gold in the interim and collecting interest. The fact that they still collect that fee and enforce the delay when it's entirely unnecessary now is (to many customers) perceived as a violation of trust.

Another example is in how many of the most profitable US companies pay extremely small amounts of taxes through what is known as a "Double Irish with a Dutch Sandwich." Using the structure of an Irish company passing funds to a Dutch company passing funds to an Irish company, Apple, Oracle, Microsoft, and IBM (which together with Google comprise the five highest-earning technology companies in the United States) had tax rates between 4.5 percent and 25.8 percent on their overseas earnings between 2007 and 2009.

In Google's case, it takes funds from search ads bought outside the United States and sends it to Google Ireland. Google mostly avoids the Irish government's corporate profit tax (at 12.5 percent) because its earnings don't stay in Ireland. Instead, they pass them to a shell company in the Netherlands as Ireland doesn't tax certain payments to companies in other European Union states. They then report a pretax profit of less than 1 percent of revenues (in 2008).

Once the money is in the Netherlands, Google takes advantage of lucrative Dutch tax laws. Google Netherlands Holdings, a shell company with no employees, then passes on roughly 99.8 percent of the cash to another shell company in Bermuda, which is technically an Irish company.

It's doubtful the above much surprises you; we're all pretty jaded to the fact that big companies are not as trustworthy or reliable as most individuals. But that doesn't change the fact that it doesn't feel fair that IKEA can avoid paying any taxes whatsoever when I have to lose such an enormous percent of my own pay just for following the rules we supposedly all decided to play by.

This same mismatch of interests is playing out online, at scale. A recent study indicated that 40 percent of social networking accounts are spam—most of which are from bots being used to push products.[1] New tools like HootSuite, Expion, Awareness, Argyle, and Shoutlet enable brands to publish content on a preset timeline. SocialFlow, Crowdbooster, Prosodic, and Adobe Social match what's being said on any given social platform and schedule the delivery of corporate content to publish at the right time to the right people to get the most exposure for their message. Platforms like VirtuOz are launching automated chat agents on platforms such as Facebook and Twitter where they act like people who are in support of specific brands.

The same thing is being done for government. In a leaked 2011 e-mail, HBGary Federal's CEO, Aaron Barr, discussed their new platforms' capabilities. "According to an embedded MS Word document found in one of the HBGary emails, it involves creating an army of sock puppets, with sophisticated 'persona management' software that allows a small team of only a few people to appear to be many, while keeping the personas from accidentally cross-contaminating each other. Then, to top it off, the team can actually automate some functions so one persona can appear to be an entire Brooks Brothers riot online." In other words, their software automatically creates fake accounts that can pass as real people and makes it easy to manage them to create the appearance of a huge groundswell of public opinion. I did mention that HBGary Federal works for the FBI, right?[2]

In each of these cases, advanced analytics, machine learning, and data aggregation are helping companies get away with pretending to be human in order to push their agendas, be that a political opinion or particular brand.[3] But just like that one weird guy who keeps trying to sell Amway at your kid's birthday party, nobody likes it. And, increasingly, everybody is starting to recognize it. As that happens our tolerance for having our social relationships milked for every last drop of profit diminishes significantly.

The problem is exacerbated when, in return, we're given roadblock after roadblock when we try to communicate in the other direction. Want to return a product? Expect complex merchandise return authorization forms, phone trees, painfully obtuse bureaucratic processes, and obscure, belittling doublespeak. But if a big organization wants access to *your* time and attention? Well, they've already got it. After all, where else am I going to go to buy a new camera except for Best Buy down the street?

The answer now, of course, is anywhere else in the world.

PATENTS AND COPYRIGHT IN THE EMERGING COMMERCIAL ECOLOGY

The problem gets worse when you start to examine how corporations have worked to shape the legal environment to suit their needs. Not that this is wrong—after all, that's what people do—but as noted, companies aren't generally very nice people because they don't have personal accountability. As individuals come to value intangibles—like trust, reputation, and relationships—that organizations cannot give them due to those values' innately personal nature, those same companies are starting to resort to dirty tricks to continue to grow. The result? A disconnect between individuals and the organizations—companies, even governments—that were developed, at least initially, to serve them.

For example, we've already talked about how disruptive 3D printing could potentially be to standard models of goods distribution. One countervailing influence against the erosion of existing markets via 3D printing that is often quoted is design patents. But Bre Pettis, founder of Makerbot, a 3D printer hugely popular with the DIY crowd, isn't concerned. "Dean Kamen has design patents on the Segway, and the police drive non-Segways all the time. Usually you get a design patent when you're monetizing something so people can't make the exact same thing. What we've seen is that derivative designs are commonly used to produce slightly revised versions, often leading to incremental improvements."[4]

Those same improvements can lead to huge gains in efficiency and price of production well beyond what the patent holder could supply. Similarly, the "value" of a design that is distributed communally often more than offsets the opportunity cost of patenting it. "When you are on Thingiverse and share something you're encouraging people to make the exact same thing because it gives you pride—your thing gets to go off to college," says Pettis. "At the same time, getting a patent is difficult, and then you have to enforce it, which is something that typically only big companies can do."

Patent law may be beneficial to big organizations that can back up their claims and throw down lawsuits to threaten off smaller competitors, but it usually has negligible value to smaller innovators and entrepreneurs. In fact, it may even be harmful. Remember, if you're engaged in reputation exchange, anything that hampers the free exchange of information limits your ability to capitalize on your investments. Patents may work very well for wealthy organizations that can use gag orders to cement their existing business models and revenue streams, but people implementing new business models and exchange systems predicated on mutual trust and access rarely benefit similarly. Even Facebook, which pioneered so many of our now-standard social software norms, tends to be less legislative than older tech companies (like Microsoft, for example), who benefit more greatly from licensing fees than from third parties adding to their platforms and building their audience. Again, it's a different business model. In the case of reputation, being transparent and available for collaboration or building on top of is a feature. In the case of "ownership" in the old sense of the word, that's often a path to loss of profit.

Here's an example of how this has played out in a more traditional industry: publishing. University of Illinois law professor Paul Heald and one of his students wrote a small program to crawl through Amazon.com and pull 2,500 random fiction titles. Then they compared the dates those books were published. What they found was that there are as many books published from the last decade as from the decade between 1910 and 1920. Why? Because works published before 1923 are no longer in copyright. Books from before then tend to be in the public domain (either by not being copyrighted or having expired out of it), and thereby avoid onerous licensing fees, and so Amazon carries them.[5]

Note that these are not used books or book sold by Amazon associates; this is what's in Amazon's warehouses right now. As Heald says, "There's as many books [that] Amazon is selling brand new right now from the 1900s to 1910 as from the 2000s to 2010. You go all the way back to 1850—there's twice as many books from the 1850s being sold on Amazon right now as the 1950s."[6] In other words, copyright means that the public gets *dramatically less* books to buy and read, because books that would otherwise be available to be freely republished (and thereby worth printing for the smaller audiences that might buy copies) are locked up in copyright, meaning that they're just not profitable investments for booksellers to reprint.

This view of the negative effect of copyright is compounded when you examine how it is used in practice in other industries and the way people are responding to it. In an article in the *Guardian*, Cory Doctorow—a well-known science fiction author, blogger, and proponent of Creative Commons (often known as copyleft) licenses—points out how the entertainment industry's strategy for media releases creates piracy.[7]

"In the empirical literature over copyright enforcement and the internet one correlation keeps resurfacing: the fewer legal options there are, the more piracy there is," says Doctorow. "If you want people to buy media, you have to offer it for sale. If it's not for sale, they won't buy it, but many of them will still want to watch or hear or play it, and will turn to the darknet to get—for free—the media that no one will sell to them."[8]

This isn't surprising. It's the same reason that iTunes was so successful once it negotiated the ability to sell songs for what they were worth to the majority of the people who wanted to buy them—along with substantial value-added services—after Napster was crushed by a Recording Industry Association of America (RIAA) intent on saving its business models from sites giving away music for free. They didn't stop piracy; they just eventually realized they needed to give listeners what they wanted for a price they were willing to pay.

A curious extension of that same mentality is that the entertainment industry forces a release schedule on its potential customers for reasons that offer no value to the customers themselves. "The US industry times blockbuster movie releases to the Thanksgiving holiday weekend (which isn't observed in the UK), the UK has bank holidays and half-terms that the US doesn't observe, so the industry has a hard time lining up the releases of all its biggest investments/cash cows with the dates on which people are most actively buying their cinema tickets," says Doctorow.[9]

The result is that a movie may come out in the United States, and suddenly be all the talk of the town online, but not be legally available in the United Kingdom for weeks or months, or vice versa. The same thing is done for TV shows, although often for different reasons. By running a season or two in the United States, producers are able to validate that the series will do well, and they can then license the property in the United Kingdom for more money. Again, it makes good business sense, but it doesn't benefit viewers whatsoever.

The result is exactly what you'd expect: People pirate the shows and movies they want to see if those shows and movies are only available illegally. What's interesting is that the way copyright law has been set up works very much to the entertainment industry's benefit because it allows them to externalize their costs by shifting the burden of enforcement to government. Instead of having to either pay to enforce their model on the market or conversely lose profit by not offering a service customers want, they're able to have the public pay tax money to have this model enforced. In other words, they're not serving their customers— they're using their political connections to make their customers pay to (literally) police themselves into adhering to an old business model rather than updating or evolving to using new technologies and new methods of media distribution. This is even more ironic given that pirating media is classified as copyright infringement

THE RISE OF THE INDIVIDUAL

which, as Doctorow points out, is a regulatory violation and not a crime.

It's an approach that isn't so surprising from a set of industries that are designed solely to subsist on control of distribution in an era when distribution costs are rapidly approaching free. But it's also desperate, and ultimately harmful. Copyright was designed originally to encourage the creation of new works, not to limit their profitability. It was created during a time when distribution of intellectual property was expensive and difficult, so creators needed to know that they would have a long enough period of time to recoup costs. But now it's often being used to sequester the profit potential to a few groups with large distribution infrastructure, while actual distribution costs are approaching zero and the return on investment period is drastically shortened through avenues like social media.

But copyright is not the only example of the misuse of existing legal controls. The patent system can be similarly damaging. Take Intellectual Ventures (IV), for example. As reported on TechDirt. com, the company, founded by Nathan Myhrvold (former CTO at Microsoft), has "used a bait and switch scheme to get a bunch of big tech companies to fund it, not realizing that they were then going to be targets of his shakedown system. Basically, IV buys up (or in some cases, applies for) tons of patents, and then demands huge cash outlays from those same companies (often hundreds of millions of dollars) for a combined promise not to sue over those patents."[10]

It's difficult to know exactly how IV operates as everyone who deals with them has to sign strict Non-Disclosure Agreements (NDAs) just to talk to them. What's more, they are able to claim that their dealings are publicly disclosed through the website of the USPTO (the patent office), which has a public database. The caveat, of course, is that the USPTO's public database is incredibly difficult to use and produces very poor results.

Fortunately, a group called PlainSite decided to apply some computational muscle to the problem in an attempt to find out what IV was actually doing. It's a classic example of a small group using technology as leverage against an established, larger entity. As reported by TechDirt, "after digging through the database, PlainSite has identified—and released for all your enjoyment—the names of what appear to be over 2,000 shell companies."

Why does IV have so many shell companies? Shell companies are traditionally used to hide the actual actions of a company, either for tax mitigation or to avoid having the competition discover what a company is doing. TechDirt hypothesizes that "what IV is almost certainly worried about is that, if the extent of its activities were known, there would be more fodder for real and necessary reform against [patent] trolling—and, more importantly, it's worried about tipping off the companies it's about to go after. It's not about competition—it's about avoiding a smart company going to court to get a declaratory judgment against IV."

In other words, IV is doing very well gaming the patent system. As a corporation, that makes a lot of sense—its bad reputation doesn't do it any harm in threatening smaller innovators. In fact, the opposite may well be true; as it gets known for destroying competitors through its proficiency in wielding patent law, it makes less and less sense for innovators and inventors to attempt to compete. It's an inverse example of the exact same motivator that reputation systems provide for individuals. Rather than making IV more well regarded, more likely to be invited to partner, license, or collaborate, their fearsome reputation ensures that only large companies with equally powerful teams of lawyers are likely to fight back.

So far this is working out well for them. After all, as long as patent law stays the same they'll be able to use their increasingly rich patent portfolio to edge out competitors—innovators and entrepreneurs—to generate greater profit for little effort. The only people who lose, of course, are the innovators who might otherwise be willing to invest in creating businesses and technologies if they weren't afraid of getting sued by IV. Oh, and the public at large who thereby cannot benefit from their innovations.

There are signs of progress, however. Recently, General Electric announced a partnership with the small product-development startup Quirky.com to release more than 30,000 patents and technologies to Quirky's open, online, crowdsourced collaborators. The goal is to spark cobranded, app-enabled, connected devices based off the intellectual property. It's clever, and if it works it could prove a new use for otherwise unused patents to benefit more people.[11]

But this view of patent law is still very new. Meanwhile, the old uses for patent and copyright are well protected by its incumbents. Recently, Karyn Temple Claggett was elected to be the new associate register of copyright and director of policy and international affairs for the US Copyright Office—its no. 2 position. Her previous job was litigating for RIAA.[12]

TECHNOLOGY: FASTER THAN COMMITTEE

The good news is that this may all be changing. Esther Dyson is a former journalist and Wall Street technology analyst who is now a leading angel investor focused on (the effective implementation of) innovation in healthcare, transparency, information technology, biotechnology, and space.[13] She points out that, increasingly, individuals have more power than institutions. "Certainly the Internet gives individuals the power to act collectively in a way that institutions cannot, to become, in a sense, institutions themselves but without much of the cost.

"Before now, one thing the little guy didn't have is a reputation that would travel and enable him to be trusted outside his own village. But now you have institutions that vouch for people without imposing the costs of scale that organizations now create for themselves," says Dyson. "Craigslist is a great example—it still has only 40 people, and that size staff enables them to enjoy great flexibility and freedom while continuing to be an enormously popular online resource."[14]

Dyson herself is a good example. "I had a secretary for years; she did reservations, travel, accounting, bookkeeping, banking, et cetera. Now I can do that all on my own—or use Taskrabbit—to accomplish all these tasks that I could not do before on my own. Previously, you had to be part of an institution. Now you can do amazing things by leveraging what often amounts to other individuals offering services over the Internet. You can write a blog and if it's good enough get enormously wide distribution."

The same advantages that now benefit individuals are conversely turning the costs of scale into disadvantages for companies. "In many cases, except for extremely well-run companies, you have actual disadvantages of scale," says Dyson. "The only way you used to be able to get any leverage was to be attached to a large institution, which in turn helped make people more productive. But now, in many cases those productivity gains are completely used up by middle managers, complex processes, and bureaucratic overhead."[15]

While big bureaucracies are suffering from the costs of headcount, bureaucracy, and misplaced expertise, "It's the little guys that benefit from reputation systems," as Dyson says. "I don't need anyone to tell me American Express is trustworthy. The big companies already *have* reputation. But now, using Airbnb, I can say, 'I can trust this woman even though I never met her. Even though she's not Marriott, I know she's going to give me a good room.'"

This rebalancing of the power relationship between corporate interests and individuals is happening at the same time as increasingly powerful technologies are becoming available to said individuals. The result? People are starting to fight back against what they perceive as a moral vacuum on the part of the commercial interests—the brands—that they formerly felt they were allied with. This is creating entirely new business models, platforms, and consumer expectations that not only challenge the status quo, but redefine it.

Here's an example. Google has what's called a TOS—Terms of Service. This document is essentially a contract you agree to when you use their service, and it protects their interests as a business, ensuring they can make a profit from your use. Unfortunately, most users don't see it that way—to them, Google is their friend, a useful service that is also free. So when it started coming to light that Google was gathering all the data users generated and using it to sell things to them (i.e., Google's core business model), things got heated.

The "tipping point" for a widespread shift in public awareness around privacy and Google came on March 1, 2012, when Google announced a change to their privacy policy that enables the company to share data across a wide variety of services—Gmail, Google Calendar, Search, Streetview, et cetera. What's more, it also tied in data collected from embedded services in millions of third-party websites using AdSense and Google Analytics, meaning that wherever you browse—whether it's a Google service or not—they'll have a record.

The change meant that suddenly, private data collected about what you searched for last night and what web pages you visited, for example, could be compared with what you e-mailed and to whom right after. Watchdog organizations mounted an awareness campaign to encourage people to clear their Google Web History, which would disconnect your personal Gmail account from your browsing history. Unfortunately, that doesn't stop Google from continuing to collect information about your activities from that point onward, and of course didn't force them to delete the information they'd already gathered.

Google's CEO, Eric Schmidt, summed up their attitude pretty succinctly: "If you have something that you don't want anyone to know, maybe you shouldn't be doing it in the first place."[16]

This may be a legal truth for Google, but it is also a logical fallacy. If I see blood in my pee, for example, I might want to find information about what it could be a symptom of and also not want to share that information with anyone. Many users felt similarly, and some left—although most simply shrugged their shoulders, and with an unsettled feeling went back to the services they felt they simply could not live without.

Brian Kennish, a former employee of Google, did neither. He'd worked at Google for seven years, managing teams of engineers on a variety of products such as the Chrome browser and the now-dead Google Wave. While he was at it, he started to notice exactly how much data was being tracked by various services, such as Google and Facebook. Eventually, he decided to write a small browser plugin to address it. As he says on his blog:

> I noticed a virus infecting the web. Facebook widgets, mostly Like buttons, were popping up everywhere—alongside the articles I read, the music I listened to, the videos I watched. Worse, Facebook was (and is) serving these widgets off the same domain (facebook.com) as their login cookies.
>
> Being a tracking aficionado (I developed DoubleClick's mobile ad server and the, kludgy, precursor to Google's AdWords API), I recognized Facebook's strategy—collecting user browsing habits to sell to advertisers.

That night, I spent two hours writing 53 lines of JSON and JavaScript (and two more hours making a Ghostbusters-inspired logo) to inoculate my browser. I called the Chrome extension, which works by stopping the flow of personal data from third-party sites to Facebook, Facebook Disconnect.[17]

His project quickly hit the list of the top 10 most downloaded Chrome plugins. Two weeks later it had 50,000 active users. Three weeks later he quit his job at Google, going on to raise $600,000 in funding and developing Disconnect to block Digg, Facebook, Google, Twitter, and Yahoo. It's now gathering over 400,000 weekly active users, and Disconnect is going strong as a company.[18]

This tells us two things. One, people are interested in protecting their privacy, and concurrently, they are suspicious that the big companies they rely on may not have their best interests at heart. Both aspects are critical for a reputation economy, because privacy impacts your ability to manage what information you choose to share, which mitigates your value in any nonfinancially relevant transaction.

And two, it tells us there's a big market for startups that want to help users achieve this. Kennish didn't raise $600,000 because of his technical chops; he did it because he released, for free, an application that was able to be widely distributed and utilized and which demonstrated his dedication to a cause many people wanted to get behind. That made it easier for him to raise funds to make it even bigger rather than the old model of trying to sell it as a product from the get-go, which might not have generated nearly as big an audience and could have precluded him getting funding. It's another example of the new reputation economy in effect.

Lest you think Disconnect is a one-off example, see also the Calyx Institute, a privacy-only Internet Service Provider (ISP) designed solely to ensure that customers own their data and that only they can decrypt it. Nicholas Merrill, formerly the head of a New York–based ISP that won a case against the FBI and Department of Justice in court over the constitutionality of the Patriot Act, plans to launch a new nonprofit, crowd-funded ISP that will make its users' privacy the central focus.[19]

While the ISP would use every technological means at its disposal to protect its customers, including encryption and limited logging, its most important feature would be its willingness to challenge government surveillance demands of dubious constitutionality.

At first blush this might appear to be knee-jerk paranoia, except that the RIAA, the Motion Pictures Association of America (MPAA), and related content industries were recently called to task on what these organizations are calling a "graduated response" plan, which is set to have Time Warner Cable, Cablevision, Comcast, Verizon, AT&T, and others installing "black boxes" in their networks to analyze all users' Internet activities and watch for potential copyright infringement. Users who are "caught" infringing on a protected work can have their service shut off and a notice provided saying that piracy is forbidden by law and carries penalties of up to $150,000 per infringement—a notice requiring the user to click and acknowledge they understand the consequences before bandwidth is restored. Regardless of whether they choose to restore service or not, they could still be subject to copyright infringement lawsuits. That means that, potentially, if your young son borrows your phone and downloads an unlicensed Shakira video, you might be out of a phone—and $150,000.

Effectively, because all of your traffic goes through your ISP, they're the perfect place to watch all your traffic, whether you want it to be private or not, and then report you to the authorities in case they don't like what they see. Suddenly, a privacy-oriented ISP seems like a really good—and profitable—idea.

But it's not just profitable new businesses that are being created out of this consumer dissatisfaction. The same impetus that drove Kennish to create Disconnect and Merrill to found the Calyx Institute is prompting other groups to make their own solutions to similar problems. In April 2012, six of the largest UK broadband providers—Virgin Media, Everything Everywhere, Sky, O2, Be, and TalkTalk—were ordered to implement server-level blocks to prevent their 13 million customers from reaching Piratebay.org, a magnet link site for bittorrenting. BitTorrent (a protocol for downloading bits of a file from millions of people simultaneously, essentially removing the centralized location of the file as a target for shutdown) is currently one of the most popular ways to download large files online, both legal—such as Creative Commons licensed books and music and Open Source Software packages—and illegal—like the latest *Pirates of the Caribbean* movie.

The bill took months to put together. It required countless hours of work on the part of legal teams, marketing divisions, political committees, and more. Strong-arming the ISPs to accept the cost—which certainly didn't win them any fans among their users—must have cost millions of pounds in favors, meetings, and lobbying. But the UK courts pushed it through, and at noon on June 19, 2012, the ISPs enacted it, meaning that roughly a third of all Internet users in the United Kingdom suddenly received an "Error—site blocked" message if they typed "www.thepiratebay .org" into their browsers.

Twenty minutes later The Pirate Bay had added two new IP addresses to their Doman Name System (DNS) records and all those users could get through again. What's more, because The Pirate Bay is using IPv6, a more advanced system for defining the addresses of their websites, they can do that same trick another 18,446,744,073,709,551,616 times, each time within minutes of any block being put in place.

The effort on the part of The Pirate Bay is minimal—it's a couple lines of code, and they could automate the process if they cared to. Even if they didn't want to be bothered, running a search for "how to access Pirate Bay" turns up 13,700,000 results (today), including videos, online services, applications and tools, how-tos, and more. All that is required to circumvent blocked IP addresses is to use a proxy or Virtual Private Network (VPN), which basically skips around your ISP's network. In Sweden, where The Pirate Bay has been blocked on and off for years, there has been a huge rise in VPN use over the past few years for exactly this reason.

This kind of casual, techno-superior response to a political act is by no means confined to people who want to download movies. A great case in point is the SOPATrack application, a free program designed to show connections between campaign donations and voting records. It was created in response to the SOPA bill—the Stop Online Piracy Act—which was being rushed through Congress at the time the app was made. SOPA was designed to expand US law enforcement's ability to fight online trafficking in counterfeit goods and copyrighted intellectual property by allowing them to request court orders to force advertising networks, payment facilities, search engines, or ISPs to stop allowing their users to connect to certain sites. In effect, it was designed to do what the United Kingdom wanted to do to The Pirate Bay, but to any site, any time any law enforcement official felt like it. Furthermore, the law would have expanded existing criminal laws to include unauthorized streaming of copyrighted content with a maximum penalty of five years in prison; even if you don't download it to your machine, just watching it could cost you five years in jail.

The online community responded in force. Wikipedia (the fifth most popular site on the Internet) blacked out all its content in protest, and hundreds of other sites followed suit. Companies from Google to Reddit pressured lobbyists to shut down the bill. SOPATrack was one of many, many responses, this one built in a single day at a Hackathon (a day-long festival where coders make applications) with these goals:

1) Help voters find their local congresspeople on any connected device
2) Allow voters to contact their members of Congress by phone or social networking site
3) Show whether a congressperson supported or opposed this issue
4) Show how much money the congressperson raised both for and against the "Stop Online Piracy Act"/"E-PARASITE Act" (SOPA) and the "PROTECT IP Act" (PIPA)[20]

It used freely available data from MapLight and free Application Programming Interfaces (APIs) from SunlightLabs, and was put online for free as soon as it was completed. The site was immediately popular, receiving coverage in the *Atlantic*, Mashable, Lifehacker, and Hacker News. Twitter, Facebook, and Google drove most of the traffic, which peaked at over 40,000 unique daily visitors. It was a simple platform using free technology and data, but the effect has been transformational: All of a sudden, any congressperson raising money around any particular issue has zero chance of it going unnoticed by his or her constituents. That's a major change in business as usual, by anyone's measure, and has significant impact on how, when, and for what congresspeople are now willing to gather funds.

This change happened overnight, took very little resources to execute, and has enormously far-reaching implications for how governance will be done from now on by destroying, overnight, the semi-anonymity of congresspeople raising funds.

Another great example is Buycott, an app for your smart-phone that allows you to scan the barcode on any product to trace the product's ownership all the way to its top corporate parent company—including conglomerates like Koch Industries, who have been widely criticized for their role in affecting climate change policy in the United States. The idea is to make it easy for people to boycott big companies with practices that violate their moral principles—rather than just their subsidiaries. The app also allows you to make or join campaigns to boycott—or buy—products made by specific types of companies depending on your politics or values.

IN TRUST WE BUY

Really, it all comes down to trust. Edelman, an independent global PR firm, has studied "trust" for several years, producing a "barometer" report on the state of trust in business, governments, and media. In 2012, the Edelman Trust Barometer showed for the first time that trust and transparency are more important to corporate success than a company's assets. Disconnect, the Calyx Institute, Buycott, and all the rest are simply embodiments of an ongoing trend in consumers' expectations about the institutions whose services they use. What's changed is that whereas in the past consumers could have liked it or lumped it, now they're able to take action or find alternatives when they don't like what they see.

Again and again, individuals are proving that they have the technological capacity to simply route around enormously expensive, unwieldy, undesirable governmental regulations and corporate policies in order to preserve and advance their reputation economies. In the process, they're building profitable new companies, platforms, and business models, many of which just happen to destroy existing systems. It's a radical departure from business as usual, and it isn't going away. If anything, it's happening faster than ever.

CHAPTER 5

THE PANOPTICON AND THE RUNAWAY CULTURE ECOLOGY

THE STRANGE OWNERSHIP OF REPUTATIONAL CONTEXT

The reason this battle is being fought isn't because big business is doing badly. Actually, it's rather the opposite. The technologies we have available to us now are making us more powerful than ever, true—but so far it's primarily been large organizations with significant resources who've mobilized them. In order to explain why there's such a war afoot we need to back up and talk a little about you—and the information companies have about you, and why their opinion that they know what they're doing with it is so very, terribly wrong.

Reputation thrives because of context. Just like that one lady you run into on the subway platform every weekday around 9 a.m., repetition and exposure breed familiarity and provide you with numerous samples with which to make an assessment. It's inaccurate (albeit easy) to judge someone from just one exposure, meaning that the more context you have, the higher confidence you can have in that evaluation.

Increasingly, *the Internet* is providing this context. From your eBay seller rating to your Yelp comments to your blog posts, there's a lot of data for people to judge you by. StackOverflow.com, a website for technologists to comment on each other's requests for help—and on which the best answers are then voted up—is often cited on a programmer's resume. Why? Because it provides an instant sample of their skills as vetted by their peers. The more useful, accurate answers you provide, the more well known and respected you are for your input. Your reputation becomes more valuable. That value can take lots of forms, from being invited to participate in development projects, to being given access to different code repositories, to being asked to act as an "expert" at conferences or on panels. This sort of instant peer review and accessible and contextualized reference is becoming commonplace on all kinds of platforms, meaning that you're suddenly able to make high-confidence judgments about otherwise complete strangers.

Within limited constraints that context is superbly useful, such as with StackOverflow. But increasingly this data is available across multiple platforms, social contexts, and sources—and yet we expect our computers to make quick work of it anyway. This easy, intuitive trust in data is what makes the transition we're in as a species—from data-scarcity to data-abundance—so dangerous. The data we're gathering isn't being normalized (rendered comparable), the models we're making aren't tested or reviewed (witness Klout as a standard for influence), and, most crucially, the information itself isn't democratically available. Small groups of people hold all the data, make all the models, and intuitively (not necessarily scientifically) interpret all the results. That's not a formula for accurate estimations of any kind, let alone for designations of relative human value. Instead, it's pretty much a recipe for disaster.

Put more specifically, all this data is being processed by models that are inherently incomplete, and often grossly inaccurate. And yet we're depending on them to convey to us accurate estimations of reality. That would be ok if we knew up front that they were faulty or based on limited data—then we could use them to adjust our own gut feeling or compare them to other results. But increasingly, they're producing startling results as a result of the amount of data we're able to put into them, and we're confusing those results for omniscience. We're falling in love with our own technology, and the results are frequently turning out to be pretty ugly.

HOW MUCH DATA IS GATHERED ABOUT YOU IN A DAY?

To get an idea of exactly how far-reaching these technologies are, let's do a quick review of how data is gathered about you in real life. (We'll come back to how and how much data is collected about you online in a bit.) On any hypothetical day, you might leave your apartment and get recorded by at least one (but probably more) CCTV cameras before you're even out of the lobby. Then street cameras record you. Of course, by then your phone has already registered your movements with your cellular provider, and any location-aware apps you have running as well. Your car starts up and its GPS registers where you are and, if it has a networked mapping function, where you're going. Or, if you take the bus, your idle conversation with the lady sitting next to you is recorded and scanned for interesting content.[1] You drop by the store to grab some last-minute items and while you're there, cameras register that you went straight to the coffee bar. Bluetooth sensors attempt to identify your phone. RFID sensors track your purchases as you carry them from the back of the store to checkout, and hidden infrared cameras monitor your eye movements as you go, tracking each product you look at and for how long. Store cameras using machine vision may attempt to determine if you're doing price comparisons on your phone along the way, if you touch a particular product before you put it down, if you're smiling when you *do* pick it up. Eventually you get to the checkout counter and use your coupon card—or not—either way resulting in your identity and purchase being logged through either the discount card network records or your credit card history (both of which are regularly bought and sold).

Congratulations, you've now almost made it to work. Now imagine you'd traveled by air, in which case one of the new picosecond programmable lasers may have been put in place. It's able to determine how much caffeine you've ingested, what you had for breakfast (and dinner last night), your heart rate, skin temperature, and more—instantly—along with everybody else in a 50-meter radius.[2]

Sound like some far-future paranoid delusion? Maybe. But at the moment all the technologies mentioned above are already in use, and their scope is getting wider every day. It is becoming, in many real ways, a panopticon, a concept coined by English philosopher and social theorist Jeremy Bentham in the late eighteenth century. The idea is that of an institutional building designed to allow a watchman to observe all the inmates of an institution without them being able to tell whether or not they are being observed. It's an interesting idea for our modern times, especially as sensors become more pervasive.

But that's not why I bring it up—the democratic impact of a global panopticon is the subject for another book. Instead, just imagine exactly how much data is being gathered about you by all those sensors, and then take a guess at how much of it is being shared (or, more likely, sold) between the companies doing the gathering. If you guessed "all of it" you're correct, and that's important.

IDENTITY VS. AUTHENTICITY: AN INTERNET USER'S PRIMER

Let me stop for a moment to explain something that is very often misunderstood about our lives online. This might get a little bumpy if you haven't spent a few decades examining issues of cryptography and Internet systems topology. Hang with me, though—if you can understand the difference between Identity and Authenticity you'll be far ahead of most of your peers in seeing how and why these new social platforms seem a little weird, and more critically you will be much better able to use them effectively.

Very often people go online and make accounts on Instagram or Vine or Path or whatever new social platform they happen to have taken a liking to and then think, "There! I've put myself online, and now people can find me and have a relationship with me."

This is not actually what is happening.

Similarly often, people (possibly you) go online and make an account that bears very little to no resemblance to themselves, and then think, "There! I've now made a completely fake account where I can pretend to be someone else, and now nobody will ever connect this account with me."

This is also not actually happening.

The last thing that occurs, and occurs often, is that both of the above people (who might, coincidentally, be the same person) then go and exchange goods and services and opinions and messages with other people with whom they then establish a relationship.

This actually does happen all the time.

However, as these people are having all these exchanges, they are very often confused about who is exchanging what with whom. That's because *who you are* (your identity) and *how people know you* (your authenticity) are programmatically different, and online that difference has profound ramifications.

An analogy might be your physical address versus a post office box. If I have your address, I can go to your house and wait in your driveway to have a conversation about how your political beliefs are morally incorrect. If I only have your post office box, at best I can send you a sternly worded letter which you are free to ignore.

The Internet is designed in such a way that this sort of representational shorthand is built-in. The URL of a website— www.gmail.com, for example—is actually a long version of the *actual* address of the machine that runs Gmail (74.125.228.53). However, 74.125.228.53 is hard for human beings to remember, so the domain name system was built to run on top of it so we could type human-readable terms like "www.gmail.com" instead. Type either into your browser and it will still turn up the correct web page.

This matters because whereas 74.125.228.53 is the actual number of a particular physical machine that you could (theoretically) track down to some data center in the real world, www.gmail.com can be changed to point to any server anywhere on the globe in very short order. The reason I bring this up is that the system was built this way exactly for the same reason that some people have post office boxes. It didn't happen by accident. That mentality pervades the online world and all the systems that are designed to support it, and it explains why the concept of identity and authenticity are important when it comes to making transactions on the web.

By way of illustration, let's say you wanted to buy some potentially embarrassing product—a "marital aid," for example. And let's say I happened to have some marital aids for sale, but didn't really want that to become public knowledge either. Discretion is the better part of valor, and all that.

The way it works in the "real world" is that I have an identity—Josh Klein, who lives at such-and-such an address, with such-and-such bank account and such-and-such social security number, et cetera. And so do you. And once we've both confirmed the real-world identity of the other, we can move money from your bank account to mine.

The problem here is that, as a side effect, you now know me and that I sell marital aids and I know you and that you buy them—and so does the bank, the FBI, and anyone else who happens to have access to the transaction records. (Which, if you've been paying attention, could be rather a lot of people.)

So instead of setting yourself up to receive a bunch of cata-
logs featuring marital aids (whether I decide to send them to
you or some other entity further down the line does), we use
authentication.

Authentication is a way of saying, cryptographically (which
means using math, which can be proven to be true), that I am
the same person who did some other thing. One way to think
of it is that I can come to you and demonstrate, mathematically,
that a user called "dragonrider15" on Facebook is also the
same guy who posted some really great pictures of architecture
on Flickr under the account name "AwesomesauceBldgPics,"
is also the same person who got a stellar rating as a car driver
on Uber under the name "HonestAbeDriver," is also the
same person who sold a bunch of collector's edition tooth-
picks on eBay with a five-star seller rating under the name
"TopNotchPickers."

This is possible because of how cryptography works,
which I won't try to explain here because it's complicated
and much messier than the point I'm trying to describe. So
for now, just take it as writ that you can run some algorithms
and *authenticate* each of those accounts as being owned by
the same account holder.

Being able to do that suddenly allows a whole bunch of
transactions to occur in ways that couldn't otherwise. So in
this case, you could come to me and say, "Hey, I want to buy
one of your marital aids, but I don't want to tell you who I
am or how to find my house or anything else. I know this
probably seems a little dodgy to you, so here's some validated evidence that I posted these messages on this forum, or
paid these bills, or otherwise met my promises in a way that
should convince you to trust me."

This is helpful, because the next time I send a message to dragonrider15, I know it's the same person receiving it as the *last* time I sent a message to dragonrider15. And if I send a message to AwesomesauceBldgPics, I can reference that message and expect that the recipient will know what I'm talking about. See where this is going?

Essentially, it means you can build reputation and trust between two people without them ever knowing the other's real-world identity. This is a powerful thing, because it allows those of us who make accounts on social platforms to verify to others that we're the same person contributing each time. Whether we're doing this "as ourselves" or if we're pretending to be some aspect of ourselves (or somebody else entirely) doesn't really matter anymore; all of a sudden we can choose to allow our actions to have accountability and continuity in a way that would have been otherwise impossible.

The caveat, of course, is that it means that people interacting with you online *don't actually know who you are*. This is both a feature and a bug. Unless you post pictures of your house, list your bank account number, or post your social security number and photo, there's no reason for people to take it as fact that you are who you say you are. Conversely, just because someone says that in real life they're a dog doesn't mean we need to believe them. In both cases, we're dealing with simple mathematical authentication of an account and the continuity it enables.

Using authentication as the primary means of validating ownership of an account also means that people can have an otherwise unprecedented level of privacy online while still participating socially in a fully functional way. If you can connect my Flickr, Facebook, Uber, LinkedIn, and eBay accounts, and I act like a total dick on one of them, you're going to be able to say nasty things about me on all the others. I probably don't want that, and the more time and effort I invest in any one of those accounts, the more I'll want to prevent that from happening by not being rude on any of them. This is useful, say, if you want to buy something from me and would like some assurance up front that I won't renege on the deal. At the same time, if I want to write some reviews of a particular marital aid, I can do so using an account that's not connected to any of the others and be confident in my privacy on the topic.

A very useful side effect of this linking is that people who authenticate their accounts with lots of evidence that they've participated willingly within them—be they on LinkedIn or Facebook or Twitter or anything else—appear more trustworthy, because they have more to lose. That's reputation.

It also means that I can use reputation to decide whom to trust *without* having to know where they live or who their family is. This may seem like it's inviting crime, but it's also making life a lot harder for human rights abusers, dictators, violent stalkers, and child predators, so don't turn up your nose just yet. The ability to have privacy while enabling reputation is a cornerstone of what's made the Internet so great. It allows us to dip our toes in the water, and if things go south we can drop the account with little repercussion. Conversely, if we really invest, then that account can accumulate value that can then become exportable to other platforms and be used to hold us accountable within its social context.

It's a nice bit of magic that's hard-coded into how the Internet works, and it's making a big difference in our ability to conduct commerce with other people around the globe.

DATA, AGGREGATED

So we know there is more data about you in the world than ever before. So what? There's lots of water in the ocean, too, and that's not bothering any of the fish.

The reason this matters is that we're now able to find the one droplet in the ocean that can solve your problem—or create it. It's difficult to get your head around exactly how specific—and far-reaching—this capability can be, or how seismically it is shifting every aspect of commerce. What if I could guess what you're going to have for breakfast tomorrow and ensure that I could do so with at least 87.6 percent accuracy? Statistically it's not implausible, especially if I have access to your credit card data and Google records. Increasingly, marketers do.

The impact of this is widespread in the extreme, especially because to date we've been very generous with this data. As outlined in the last chapter, we're giving away our personal information whether we like it or not simply by interacting with the very tools we need to do our jobs and live our lives; it's the nominal cost of existing online.

But most critically, the difference is that all that data used to float around separately. Our tax records weren't correlated with our Amazon.com wish list, which wasn't correlated with our browsing history, which wasn't correlated with our Facebook wall. Now it is. And the fact that it no longer takes a human being to translate that information into the maximum marketable price for a given product *for you* spells a big change in how commerce happens.

Put another way: Tools now exist to take all of the billions of bits of information that you're generating every second and translate it all into accurate estimations about your behavior, desires, and likely actions that you cannot possibly predict for yourself. It's the ultimate instance of your reputation preceding you.

A COMPREHENSIVE PICTURE OF YOU

All that information could be useful to you if you controlled it, but you don't. Companies do, and all that data aggregated together composes a startlingly accurate picture of you and your activities. A perfect example is Spokeo.com. Spokeo popped up on the Internet around 2006 and for a while was the straw man of privacy advocates everywhere (until Facebook's then-new privacy policy came out and wildly overshadowed it as the bad boy on the block). What's interesting about Spokeo is that it didn't do anything all that unique. It basically gathered publicly available information from a variety of sources—US tax records, Google street view, Twitter, et cetera—and put it all in one place. It's a function that numerous enterprise-level applications had been fulfilling for years, albeit only for large companies, mostly to help advertisers looking to improve their targeting or insight on particular customers.

What Spokeo did that so offended people was commodify this data and make it widely available. Whereas before all that information was available in bits and pieces, Spokeo offered a compiled dossier on any identity for $3 per month. Again, this is nothing new—these compilations had been available to companies for years. But by turning around and making it available to anyone, Spokeo suddenly exposed exactly how much information was really out there and how readily anyone could access it.

And it's a *lot* of information. If I have your e-mail address, or your name and the city you live in, or your Twitter handle, or any of a dozen different types of identifying data, I can get your:

- home address
- average income
- number, age, sex, and names of household members

- family structure (number of children, identity of your spouse, et cetera)
- phone number
- pictures of your house
- neighbor's likely ethnicity
- religion
- map of your neighborhood
- Facebook, Twitter, LinkedIn, Flickr, or other social software accounts
- ...the list goes on and on

Put another way, if I wanted to stalk you and ruin your life, I could do it very effectively after a single query on Spokeo, and that scared the bejesus out of a lot of people. The fact that companies have had this data and were using it to sell things to people who didn't want them and had been for years seemed rather secondary. After all, Amazon charges people differently based on their ZIP code and has for a long time, and so far nobody has seemed to much care about or even be aware of it.

Here's another example to think about. Facebook owns Instagram, the photo-sharing platform, as well as Face.com's proprietary algorithm for facial recognition. If you've got both the Facebook and Instagram apps on your phone, tablet, or laptop, Facebook has access to unique identifier numbers for both the device and for the individual installations of each app. Facebook can also cross-reference faces between Facebook and Instagram. Because Facebook heavily encourages people to use their real name, Facebook can attribute identity in several ways both to Instagram accounts and to images. In other words, Facebook likely owns the world's largest set of analyzed faces associated with names, along with a huge set of data about the relationships between those names. If you let either app have access to location information, Facebook can also attribute your physical world location, your movement, and the content of your communication. So now Facebook has a very good chance to know where you are, what you're doing there, and who you're talking to about it as long as someone snaps a picture of you that features your face and posts it on the Internet—even if you don't use Facebook.

This sort of data aggregation and analysis is happening across *all* the major platforms. Skype, now owned by Microsoft, was recently exposed as reading everything you type in a Skype chat session. This is entirely legal; it's covered in their terms of service. But they also seem to follow web links you send, especially ones that include login information. Again, this is probably legal, but it isn't very nice, and it's certainly a great way for them to get some pretty personal information about you.[3] It's not just big platforms like Skype, either. Bloomberg terminals, the famously protected computer systems designed for finance professionals to monitor and analyze real-time financial market data and place trades, also monitors its users. Bloomberg employees can see how many times each function was used, the date and time that any customer last logged into his terminal, transcripts of chat sessions, and more.[4]

This goes beyond purely corporate use. An immigration reform measure recently passed by the Senate creates a national biometric database of basically every adult in the country, linking name, age, social security number, and photograph with a driver's license or other state-issued photo ID. The implications for this are huge—as an example, employers may be required to look up every new hire in the database to verify that they match their photo. The real question is, what happens when that database gets linked to Facebook? Or LinkedIn? Or Spokeo?[5]

But this level of data aggregation is even more concerning when you consider all the information being gathered by those sensor networks I mentioned earlier, because so far it hasn't been integrated very widely. It's one thing to know that you live in Bellevue, Washington, that your home is worth $350,000, and that you have a son who is three years old. It's quite another to know those things *and* to be aware that on two separate occasions you went into a particular clothing store and picked up a pink dress for infants age 0–6 months and smiled before gently touching your belly.

That's where we're headed now. The same aggregation that we've seen happen online is creeping over into the real world in a powerful new way—powerful because our civic structures, unlike the fundamental underpinnings of the Internet, are *not* designed for democratic information sharing. As the ever-eloquent John Gilmore put it, "The internet detects censorship as damage, and routes around it."[6] All the data we're putting online is operating in an ecosystem designed to maximize free information exchange and sharing, which is how systems like Spokeo pop up just as easily as ones like Ushahidi, which mashes up Google maps and online chat rooms to allow volunteers to search for survivors in pictures of post-earthquake Haiti from thousands of miles away. In other words, the essentially open nature of the Internet has acted as a countervailing force to essentially corporatized centralization efforts all along.

But the physical world is much more tightly managed by the people who actually install the cameras, RFID sensors, cell phone systems, and so forth. And those controlling entities can make quite different decisions about who to share their data with than a server on the Internet. Specifically, they can sell all that data to a closed network of buyers, meaning that not only will you never get access to that data about you, you'll never even know it existed in the first place.

That makes certain circumstances suddenly seem a lot more likely—like your insurance premium unexpectedly getting hiked up because a machine-vision system connected to a traffic cam saw you in a car with someone in the driver's seat that it facially mapped and recognized as having high premiums themselves.

More significantly, it means that a big part of your public profile as companies see it will remain invisible to you, which is doubly important when you consider exactly how smart their models about you really are. They're very smart, and disastrously often very wrong, and that's because of...

MAKING SAUSAGE: CHURNING DATA INTO MEANING

We've seen in numerous studies that people wildly overestimate how much their daily routines vary. We're all a lot more predictable than we like to think. And it turns out that the larger the sample size, the more accurate the models that result from the survey. Put together all the data collected by sensor technologies and online aggregators, and you've got a *lot* of data being collected about a *lot* of people, which makes for some pretty accurate models indeed. (Accurate, and often mistaken—more about this in a later chapter.)

Just as a quick reality check, keep in mind that a company like Google only needs 22 points of data to specify a discrete identity. So when you're browsing on your laptop, Google can then connect that with your phone when you're shopping and check a price on an item in a store. Google doesn't necessarily need you to be logged in, either: It has code that observes all the user behavior on any site it resides on, collecting all kinds of data points it can then use to identify you. That data point could be as small as the average time between clicks or the order in which you move between websites.

Much like Spokeo took publicly available information outlets (such as those provided by the US government about tax records, or name and phone number information provided by the white pages) and brought them all together, now new companies are going even deeper in pulling together ever-broader data canons. Infochimps.com, for example, processes terabytes of data a day from hundreds of different sources, from Twitter to Facebook to that Yahoo chat group you just posted to. A terabyte is 1,024 gigabytes, or 1,048,576 megabytes, or 1,099,511,627,776 bytes. An average tweet is a maximum of 560 bytes, so that means Infochimps is processing a large multiple of 1,963,413,621 tweets worth of data per day. They've wrapped all this data in the very latest APIs, so it's readily accessible to programmers. They've normalized all the data so you don't have any junk to wade through. They've provided prebuilt streaming analytics to make queries on the data easy to assess. Generally speaking, they've done everything they can to make Spokeo look like a lemonade stand in comparison to their ability to derive meaning from an enormous amount of social data about you.

And they're not alone. Online advertising is such a hot market—and its value is such an unknown quantity—that there are more companies popping up to attempt to measure, aggregate, and distill the data than you could shake a stick at. Lingia, a relatively new startup that closed a $3.5 million Series A investment round (their first significant round of venture funding), identifies the most active users in a particular category and contacts them to share a particular story. It finds the most popular blogger, commenter, journalist, or participant for any niche—say, toast sculpture—and offers them money to say nice things about a product—say, a spatula.

What's interesting about it is its scale—Lingia apparently has access to millions of small, discrete groups and makes it easy for companies to target any niche they want, meaning marketers no longer have to spend their time participating in those small groups themselves. It hits the mid- to long-tail (i.e., where a small number of people buy a product, but where there are many, many types of product which in aggregate create a large amount of goods sold). This lets companies avoid the megaphone approach and instead cater content specifically to each niche—and lets them do it by the hundreds of thousands of potential customers. All of which suddenly seems frighteningly plausible when you consider exactly how much data about those customers is actually available.

At the same time, companies are spending a whole lot of time turning all that data into meaning. As an example, Xerox now leaves all hiring for its 48,700 call center jobs to software. In a six-month trial period, they found that a 30-minute online personality test that asks applicants to choose between statements like "I ask more questions than most people do" and "People tend to trust what I say" cut attrition by a fifth. It turns out that their HR team's assumptions about what did and did not constitute a good applicant were demonstrably, statistically, and reliably wrong.[7]

By having applicants take variants of the test and then tracking their performance, the software developers were able to create a very accurate model of what an optimal applicant looked like. Because it's statistically generated, it can continue to be improved over time as all the data on the hired employees continues to be gathered, meaning it will only become more refined for—and better at predicting—that definition of "ideal employee."

Xerox isn't alone—globally, spending on this kind of talent-management software increased to $3.8 billion in 2011, up 15 percent from 2010, according to Gartner research.[8] And it's easy to see why. Instead of having a human being sit down with another human being and ask them questions, you can just have an applicant spend 30 minutes filling out a web form and voila! Out comes a hiring decision.

Of course, there are external considerations. Systems like the one Xerox uses may find that older applicants generally make worse employees and discriminate against them—despite that being against the law. That sort of moral consideration is outside the scope of the algorithm, but it is equally un-ignorable. It's also a pretty good example of why all this data represents a big problem, because as we attempt to make sense of it we're going to attach certain assumptions to our algorithms that produce outcomes we may or may not like.

But before we get into that, let's take a look at exactly how we *are* trying to make sense of all this data, and what the technologies are like that we're using to do it with.

A/B TESTING: THE PRESIDENCY'S CODE WAR

The technology being used to do this is often complex, but there are a few aspects of its use that are readily understood by mere mortals. By way of example, take A/B testing, an absolute staple of any successful online service you've ever used.

A/B testing is a straightforward concept. You make two versions of something and test how different sets of users respond to each. If I were selling lemonade, I could color one pitcher pink and one pitcher yellow and sell them both to similar sets of audiences to see which made more money. Now broaden the scope. Let's say I could employ infinite numbers of six-year-olds to create infinite variations of lemonade—colors, amount of ice, percent of sugar versus lemon juice, et cetera. Now scale it out so you could test each variation with a statistically significant number of potential lemonade buyers—say, a thousand people for each lemonade formula. Finally, imagine that I could do all of these tests at the same time, and could keep doing them, making slight changes based on the results all along the way, in perpetuity. The result is a rapid, iterative process in which minor changes churn their way to the "best" solution—with very little human intervention, and usually in mere hours. Welcome to the Internet.

This technique is used online by everything from e-commerce sites to chat forums. Any change at all—background color, button position, text—can be tested immediately to produce useable, statistically analyzed information that can be immediately applied to help drive success. What's more, any user behavior that can be measured can be used to test against. Want to keep your visitors on your site longer? You can gather that data. How about purchases? Or registrations? Or click-throughs? Or video plays? All of it can and is being optimized, continuously.

Brian Christian posted about this on *Wired* on April 25, 2012, and provided a great example of how it plays out.

After joining the Obama campaign, Siroker [a digital advisor working on the campaign] used A/B to rethink the basic elements of the campaign website. The new-media team already knew that their greatest challenge was turning the site's visitors into subscribers—scoring an email address so that a drumbeat of campaign emails might eventually convert them into donors. Their visit would start with a splash page—a luminous turquoise photo of Obama and a bright red "Sign Up" button. But too few people clicked the button. Under Siroker's tutelage, the team approached the problem with a new precision. They broke the page into its component parts and prepared a handful of alternatives for each. For the button, an A/B test of three new word choices—"Learn More," "Join Us Now," and "Sign Up Now"—revealed that "Learn More" garnered 18.6 percent more signups per visitor than the default of "Sign Up." Similarly, a black-and-white photo of the Obama family outperformed the default turquoise image by 13.1 percent. Using both the family image and "Learn More," signups increased by a thundering 40 percent.[9]

The part that shocked Obama's team most was just how off their instincts were during the test. Almost 100 percent of the staffers thought a video of Obama speaking at a rally would totally outperform any still photo. But the video fared 30.3 percent *worse* than any image—even the beloved turquoise one. If the team had listened to its instincts and kept "Sign Up" as the button text while simultaneously swapping out the photo for the video, the signup rate would have dropped to 70 percent of the baseline. Even worse, without the controls and rigorous data collection A/B testing offered, the team never would have known why the numbers fell and would have attributed it to some drop in favor for Obama instead of a bad site revamp.

"Instead, when the rate jumped to 140 percent of baseline, the team knew exactly what, and whom, to thank," the article continued. "By the end of the campaign, it was estimated that a full 4 million of the 13 million addresses in the campaign's email list, and some $75 million in money raised, resulted from Siroker's careful experiments."

A/B testing is ubiquitous on most successful sites today and is an absolute staple for web developers everywhere. The result is that, oddly, nothing we see online is "the" page or service—it's almost always a subtle variation designed to test your response to a minor change. This ongoing, iterative, evolving approach to developing services is in many ways similar to Darwin's theory of evolution. Successful designs thrive, and failed ones fade away. In this case, however, the successes are the ones that change your behavior to produce the desired result.

BAYESIAN FILTERING (FINDING LOVE FOR GEEKS)

A/B testing is just the tip of the iceberg, however. While it can and does generate useful data that can be immediately put to use, it's not quite as exciting as the near-prescience I described at the start of this chapter. To do that, we have to look at Machine Learning.

Machine learning, as described by Wikipedia, is "a scientific discipline concerned with the design and development of algorithms that allow computers to evolve behaviors based on empirical data, such as from sensor data or databases."[10] As noted, we now have a hell of a lot of empirical data, and there are copious toolkits and innumerable algorithms, models, and methods used to make sense of them with machine learning. The interesting bit here is in the "learning" part—in that our machines can now *evolve*.

Take Bayesian filtering. Named after Thomas Bayes (1701–1761), it "relates inverse representations of the probabilities concerning two events."[11] In plain language, it lets you take two sets of things and algorithmically infer the difference. Bayesian filtering is most famously used in spam filtering, because it lets you take two sets—spam and non-spam e-mails—and calculates the likelihood that new e-mails are either one or the other. Bayesian filtering generally gives a low rate of false positive; it rarely identifies real e-mail as spam, which makes it hugely popular as a spam filter.

This is all very handy, and I'm sure we're all very grateful. Nonetheless, I personally never gave a damn about it until I learned that it could also help you get laid. In 1996 one of the first known mail-filtering programs to use a Bayes classifier was Jason Rennie's iFile program.[12] In 2002 Paul Graham was able to greatly improve the false positive rate, and Bayesian filtering was soon thereafter deployed in any number of commercial spam filters.[13] It wasn't too long after then that the technology caught the eye of John (not his real name), a friend of a friend of mine in Seattle.

It turns out John had been poking around some of the more popular open source spam filtering packages, like Spamassassin, and had grokked that Bayesian filtering could be used for *any* set of text items. At the time he'd just broken up with his girlfriend and was despairing over the enormous investment of time required to sort out all the prospective dates he could approach via MySpace, chat rooms, and the like. The problem, as he saw it, was that there were *too many* women out there that he *didn't* want to date, and it was too difficult to tell which ones he *did*.

So he applied Bayesian filtering. Using the Spamassassin package and a little quick-and-dirty scripting, he sucked down the MySpace pages of all the girls he'd dated and liked (but that didn't work out for one reason or another) as well as the pages of all the girls he'd dated and *didn't* like. He used these to teach his Bayesian filter which ones were "spam" (the ones he didn't like) and which ones were "ham" (the ones he did).

From there he wrote another small script to grab the MySpace pages of every woman between the ages of 20 and 30 who was a friend of a friend of his and who lived within a five-mile radius. He then ran the results through his Bayesian filter.

The results were dramatic. John went from roughly 200 potential candidates to about 25, and of those 25 there were a dozen or so that he knew right off the bat might be a good match. What's more, they were all pretty geeky girls, so when he actually approached them and told them what he'd done, many of them thought it was super cool (as opposed to strictly creepy). He had six dates scheduled by the end of the week.

Bayesian filtering is just one example of hundreds of different algorithms, mathematical models, and software toolkits that compose what is currently known as machine learning. Essentially, these tools make and improve estimations based on the data supplied. As we've seen, these canons of data can be pretty enormous, and as evinced by their utility, these toolkits are evolving pretty fast. This evolution is often the most surprising aspect of the field, at least to the layman—we're used to the idea that code, once written, doesn't change. After all, evolution is a unique advantage of the human, plant, and animal world, right?

Not necessarily. In fact, one quickly evolving field in machine learning is genetic programming, in which a program actually "evolves" another program through many, many versions in order to find the one best fit for the task. Just like real-life evolution, it's resource-intensive and time-consuming, but with the computational power we have at our disposal, it is often surprisingly successful.

Often, machine learning approaches are actually more focused on this evolution than on the data itself. Neural networks, another field of machine learning that has received a lot of attention, modify their behaviors and parameters depending on the stimulus they receive. Each "state" of behavior is only kept for as long as it functions well in response to the stimulus, meaning it is constantly changing in real time, without a gigantic log of pre-prepared responses suitable for any situation. The fact that its current "model" of response is able to adapt to any input allows it to respond to inputs it has never seen before.

If there are hundreds (if not thousands) of other even more advanced tools out there—all of them using massive data canons, flexible adaptation, and evolving models of response—imagine what big companies are doing with them. Here's a hint: They're not just trying to get a date.

MACHINE LEARNING AND CREDIT CARD FRAUD

To give you an idea of how widespread and effective machine learning has become, consider credit card fraud. We've all heard lots about it and we know that it's supposedly a prime target for crime. It makes sense: Credit cards are extremely easy to use and require very little authentication. All you need is the card, and most of the time you're not even asked for evidence that you're the person whose name is on it.

So given all that, how is it that credit cards can exist at all? The answer is a little frightening, and to understand why, it's helpful to consider how much a credit card account is worth on the black market.

Yes, you can buy activated credit card numbers online. Go to the right website, and you can buy activated, verified, working credit card numbers along with all the information you need to use them—full names, addresses, CSC codes, et cetera. Usually you have to buy them in lots of hundreds or thousands, and part of the reason is that, on average, a credit card account is worth about a dollar.

One dollar.

Think about that. If you can ostensibly take out as much money as you like from a credit card, without authentication, then how is it that the value of a working, valid credit card is only a dollar? By way of comparison, a working, valid *World of Warcraft* game account goes for *six dollars*.

The answer lies with machine learning. Put succinctly, credit card companies are enormous multinational entities with absolutely massive databases of consumer behavior. They know who, what, when, and where every single credit card transaction happens anywhere on the planet. A set of data that big means that your machine learning algorithms can get smart—really smart—really quickly.

The reason credit cards are only worth a dollar on the black market is that a working credit card can only have an average of one dollar's worth extracted from it, because the credit card companies are so good at determining what a fraudulent transaction looks like. If you've ever been called by your credit card company to verify a purchase you know what I'm talking about, and chances are pretty good that when they did that, it was indeed a suspicious transaction. This is outside of those transactions that are denied outright because they seem so likely to be fraudulent and which you then had to call in to clear.

If this doesn't sound familiar to you, it's because those same algorithms are working so well that it's basically invisible—why would you have a transaction denied because it looked fraudulent when the credit card companies *know* what sort of transactions you're likely to make? What you do normally looks normal, because for you, it is. And the credit card companies know it.

The real impact of this can be driven home by considering the fact that all this is happening dynamically. You're not making the same transactions today that you were a year ago; you've changed as a person, as have your environment, your tastes, your lifestyle, maybe even your employment situation. In short, what's "normal" is a moving target when it comes to credit card transactions. And that's true for everybody who uses credit cards, which is basically the entire First World. So with that many moving targets, how's it possible that we're not all awash in continuous streams of mistakenly identified fraudulent transactions?

It's because machine learning is evolving right alongside us. In fact, if anything, it's evolving faster.

LEAPS IN SCALE THROUGH COMPUTING IN THE CLOUD

I'd like to mention one other big shift in the computational landscape that's making reputation economics possible. All of the above technologies are extremely clever, useful tools, but they all require resources. It's akin to explaining that FedEx is an amazingly efficient material goods distribution system but forgetting to talk about the fuel required to drive their trucks.

The reason I bring this up is because that fuel is essentially what cloud computing is. Not the sexy apps Google Docs provides or flashy storage systems like DropBox or SugarSync. At their most fundamental these are basically just big hard drives or programs running on top of computer systems hosted elsewhere. More important by far are the processor farms that host those drives and programs, and the cataclysmically massive power they provide.

The "horsepower" of a computer is measured in cycles—the number of computational instructions that can be processed per second. Instructions per second (IPS) is commonly used in association with a numeric value such as thousand instructions per second (kIPS), million instructions per second (MIPS), billion instructions per second (GIPS), or million operations per second (MOPS). (There are a number of mitigating factors that affect computer performance, leading to other standardized tests such as SPECint, but IPS is still a useful analogy.) Roughly put, the more "work" a computer has to do, the more instructions it has to process, which is what makes it a useful general-purpose measurement.

And nowadays there are a *lot* of instructions to process. Your phone alone runs thousands of times more instructions through it every minute than the biggest vacuum-tube computers could do in days, and that demand is universal and increasing. Remember all that data that's being collected now? A whole lot more instructions have to be run just to examine each piece of data.

The demand is *so* great that large companies such as Google and Amazon ended up making specialized data centers that ran "clusters" of computers with massive "parallel processing" capabilities—basically, each cluster acts like a single giant computer with loads of processors, enabling it to process many more instructions per second.

To give you an idea of how big this demand really is, consider Project 02, one of Google's largest data centers. It's located approximately 80 miles from Portland in The Dalles, Oregon, on the Columbia River. The $600 million complex was built in 2006 and is roughly the size of two football fields, with four-story-high cooling towers.

The entire complex is basically one giant room full of computers, all stacked one on top of the other. The power demand is so great that the site was chosen specifically because it's near a hydroelectric dam, which provides cheap electricity. And Project 02 is an *old design*. New data centers are being built all over the world, and increasingly they're being situated in Scandinavia because all those computers generate a lot of heat, and if it's always cold outside, it's a lot cheaper to cool them. According to some estimates, for every 100 watts spent on running the servers, roughly another 50 watts is needed to cool them, and if you're spending billions of watts per hour—as a company like Amazon does—there's a lot of money to save on cooling.

Having all these giant data centers located somewhere else meant that companies like Google and Amazon spent a lot of time and effort connecting those resources to the services we use today. If I search for a document on Google, it doesn't matter to me if the request is processed in Finland, Malaysia, or my backyard—I expect the result to always be nearly instantaneous.

But there's a funny thing about massive infrastructure like these—demand is not steady. Just like the electrical grid, there are "peak hours" when the system is being used more heavily, and conversely there are times when it's barely being used. So, like any good business, the companies that built these systems decided to rent out the unused cycles—and the cloud was born.

You see, as the giant megacorporations of our digital lives were expanding, new companies have been springing up alongside at an ever-increasing pace. Instagram, Twitter, Groupon—all are companies that use data and services provided by other digital entities. Most of these startups were using open-source libraries and free software packages to build services on the cheap, and the majority of them were using large quantities of data to pull out interesting services for their customers. The only problem is that they all required computational power—and they didn't have budgets.

They had the same problem Google had, except they couldn't just go and build a massive data center to test out their new wonder-program. So instead they rented only as much as they needed from services like Amazon's S3 network, knowing that if customers suddenly started flooding through their door, Amazon would automatically provide them with as much computational capability as they needed, on demand, for a price.

It turned out that this model—of only paying for what you used, instead of buying a massive data center that may never be fully utilized—was incredibly popular. Partly this was because the cost (and therefore the risk) of trying out a new digital company dropped through the floor. Whereas it had originally cost literally millions of dollars to see if a company like Twitter would succeed, it now could cost hundreds or less.

This increase in potential wasn't lost on anybody, and suddenly there was an explosion of new sites and services. The massive growth in software development prompted a concomitant boom in free and open software packages that were increasingly easy to use, which created a feedback loop by prompting more sites and services to be developed.

Single-serving sites are a great example: websites so simple they consist of only one page providing a very small bit of data. For instance, HowManyPeopleAreInSpaceRightNow.com is a simple counter that provides the total number of astronauts currently serving on the International Space Station. That's it—a number.

Before cloud computing, you would have had to buy the domain name (a more expensive proposition before demand drove the price down); buy a powerful computer; pay to get it installed in a data center with a solid Internet connection, 24/7 access, and cooling capabilities; hire someone to set up the server and then monitor the server as it operated; and then pay someone, like NASA, to give you the information to post on HowManyPeopleAreInSpaceRightNow. com. Now, you buy a cheap domain name, kick up a virtual server on Amazon or Google or whoever's cloud service you like, click on a prepackaged website software configurator, and plug in a data feed that NASA now provides for free. Copy and paste some ad code from Google and type in your PayPal account information and boom! You can start collecting cash immediately. If the site goes viral (or even becomes moderately popular) your cloud provider can automatically spin up as many instances as are necessary to support the traffic.

It's a big difference in difficulty, and the ease of access cloud computing has provided has had huge effects, not least of which is in making the Internet a massive free-for-all of services and platforms addressing every conceivable need. The real upshot of all these cheap, dynamically allocated, easy to use resources for computation, however, is that now *everyone* could use all that big data to train their machine learning algorithms and run their A/B tests effectively and on a global scale. The result has been an exponential increase in technological capability across the board, and that hasn't always been a good thing.

IT'S THE MODEL, STUPID

So we know that developers are able to iteratively test their designs to optimize our behavior to their liking. We know their programs can teach themselves to make sense of the massive amounts of data out there so they can target those designs in the first place. And we know that there is near-infinite computing power to allow them to optimize these systems on an ongoing basis. So what?

A lot of data, and the capability to make use of it to alter human behavior, means a lot of power in systems that previously didn't exist, systems that don't even have analogs to compare themselves to. These cheap, iterative, and agile new capabilities are creating exponential growth that vastly exceeds our ability to comprehend the impacts of the innovations we're making—how our creations are recursively and systemically redesigning social, economic, and cultural processes. It's a runaway culture ecology, fueled by technology we're implementing on instinct.

Put another way, we as a species are suddenly able to model, or map out, entirely new geographies of human behavior, expectation, and capability at a depth and breadth that were inconceivable a decade ago. That's where the critical point that's being missed here lies. It's in making the classic mistake of conflating our abilities with our expectations that we come to the next chapter and the fly in the ointment for the apparently godlike power that all these technologies represent. Because no matter how smart your technology is, no matter how broad the data you put into it or how deep your server clusters are, they're still going to operate on the models you define the process by. If that model is incorrect, the mistakes you make with it are as wide-reaching as the scope of the data you've based it on. Now, as ever, the map is not the territory.

CHAPTER 6
FLIES AND OINTMENTS

AUGMENT, DON'T REPLACE

n most cases there are two problems with the way companies rely on computer models as accurate representation of reality:

1) Their models are flawed, and
2) They're usually designed solely to extract only money from people, whereas people are (usually) interested in more than just money.

For now, let's focus on the first, why it's such an issue, and how adjusting our expectations could go a long, long way toward allowing us to harness the technologies we're currently so happily encouraging to run amuck. Put simply, all this computational and technological power isn't bad in and of itself, no more than a hammer is. Yes, you can kill someone with a hammer, but you can also build houses with it. Our problem is that we're so infatuated with hammers that we're giving them to our soldiers and sending them off to war. Or arming our carpenters with guns and telling them to build houses. Pick your analogy, the result is the same—bad.

Instead, we can recognize that our tools have limitations. Not so we can justify throwing them out—just because a hammer isn't as efficient at killing people as a gun doesn't mean it isn't useful. Rather, we recognize those limitations so we can *apply our tools where they're most effective.* To do that, we have to first understand why it is that all this magical new capability is built on such a shaky foundation, and what can happen as a result.

CAUSALITY IS INFINITE

Most models are flawed exactly *because* all this technological capability is enormously powerful. Like the Borg in *Star Trek*, the computers need human beings to make intuitive decisions, and when the computers get too much control they tend to make a mess of things *because* they cannot understand the numerous, dynamic, intensely human (and therefore vague and messy) elements involved. And this is why reputation is so critically noncomputational—because computers cannot model the complexity of reputation by themselves.

I'm not saying computers cannot make predictions based on reputation—after all, one of the most important elements of reputation is its role as a predictor of action. Within very narrowly defined models we can produce very accurate predictions of behavior indeed, such as with credit scores. Instead, computer models fall down hardest when they try to include multicontextual elements across a variety of domains. "Multicontextual elements across a variety of domains" describes real life, by the way, and the one human beings typically use reputation within.

Reputation requires that multiple contexts be juggled within psychosocial constructs that are constantly evolving and ever-changing. Knowing that New York City just had massive flooding because of a hurricane changes how you'll evaluate that recent tweet from a New Yorker, and as a result will change the relative value of someone retweeting that comment. That's a bit much for any computer to handle, at least for now.

A big part of the problem is that the only way we know how to work with computers (so far) is to make models of the real world as best we can, and then design our code around those models. We could model likely user behavior on an e-commerce site, or make models of financial systems that evolve over time, or even model the weather. But those models are not, and will never be, as inclusive as reality itself.

The distinction is critical. The technology itself is amazingly powerful, as are the insights it generates. But at some point the correlation between the technology and the real world starts to break down in some spectacularly harmful ways because the technology is based on models that miss some aspect of "real life" in favor of its own simplified virtual universe. Our computers are incredibly powerful tools, but they are not yet able to understand the real world in the peculiarly fuzzy, ambiguous, multicontextualized, and evolutionarily advantageous way that our brains do.

Before we examine the problems these models are causing, however, let's make clear *why* our models are so irrevocably destined to be wrong.

SIMPLE MODELS, FULL OF FAIL

There are many issues with these admittedly amazing computer models, but one of the most impactful is that causality is effectively infinite. In other words, the same complexity that allows a butterfly flapping its wings in China to create a hurricane in New York means that any model we make is incomplete—and often catastrophically so.

Part of the issue is the oversimplification of the models computer programs are based on. For example, in early April 2011, Peter Lawrence's *The Making of a Fly*, a classic work in developmental biology that many biologists consult regularly, was listed on Amazon.com as having 17 copies for sale: 15 used from $35.54, and two new from $23,698,655.93 (plus $3.99 shipping).[1]

The book, last published in 1992, is now out of print, but that hardly explains the (somewhat excessive) pricing. Instead, what had happened was that two automated programs, one run by seller "bordeebook" and one by seller "profnath," were engaging in an iterative and incremental bidding war. Once a day profnath would raise their price to 0.9983 times bordeebook's listed price. Several hours later, bordeebook would increase their price to 1.270589 times profnath's latest amount.

Keep in mind that the price had *started* at somewhere near $35, and it gives you an idea of how long this exercise in insanity had been going on. But more importantly, *why* was this happening? First off, these sorts of automated scripts are exceedingly common on e-commerce sites. eBay is rife with them, and it's effectively what Amazon does on a large scale as part of its own fundamental business model. That doesn't explain why bordeebook was *raising* the price, however—wouldn't *lowering* the price to slightly below the competition work better?

Not necessarily. De-escalating price wars are common—it's a fundamental notion of capitalism and the free market. But the bots were simultaneously smarter and more stupid than that. Both profnath and bordeebook had very high seller ratings on Amazon, and both of them can (again, automatically) buy copies for a lower price from another seller. It's a reasonable bet that for any particular book a potential customer will have a range of sellers to buy from, and a high seller rating may be worth a dollar or two more in price to the buyer if it guarantees the book arrives on time and in good condition. Put these elements together, and you have a situation where it makes sense for sellers with high feedback ratings to price books they don't own, but can get, at slightly higher than their competitors, betting on the fact that some customers will pay them more for the book based on reputation alone.[2]

It's an excellent example of how models that are well designed within understood parameters generate bad results due to unanticipated factors that were not included in the model. In this case, both sellers had made bots—automated computer scripts—that turned their reputation (their high seller rating) into cash, indulging in an automated arms race based on poorly rated influence.

It begs the question of how they got their high seller ratings in the first place, and if it was as easily gamed. Because if so, then some clever programmers are minting money by farming Amazon's reputation system. What seems more likely, however, is that more than one person just coded up a bot that didn't have sane upward limits, with absurd pricing on a few books as a result.

A similar situation arose when a T-shirt seller on Amazon. co.uk got some substantially negative feedback for selling a T-shirt emblazoned with the statement, "Keep Calm and Rape a Lot." One might wonder who thought such a shirt would be a big seller, and why, which is exactly what the twitterstorm of complaints against the seller was asking. Therein lies the big problem—most people assume a human being carefully drew up the design, commissioned a few hundred (or thousand) copies of the shirt to be printed, and carefully stored them in a warehouse before meticulously creating an Amazon page to sell them to an anticipated huge audience.

Nothing could be further from the truth. Solid Gold Bomb, the company that made the shirt, apologized copiously, but in their defense the only mistake they made was a small coding error. Not even that—it was the mistake of overlooking a single word in a list of 4,000 or so others.

That's because the shirt wasn't designed by anyone. Nor was the store "made." Nor were the shirts even ever printed. Solid Gold Bomb's business isn't really in making websites to sell shirts, or even in producing T-shirts. Instead, they write code that takes libraries of words that slot into popular phrases (such as "Keep Calm and Carry On," which enjoyed a brief mimetic popularity online) to make derivations that get dropped onto a template of a T-shirt and automatically get posted as an Amazon item for sale.

Again, nobody made the T-shirt. If anyone had bought it, their code would have automatically submitted the design to a printer somewhere, who would have then shipped it on Solid Gold Bomb's behalf. It cost them close to nothing to create the design and put it up on Amazon, and nothing for Amazon to host it (or near enough to nothing for anyone to care). If nobody bought the shirt, then the experiment effectively cost nothing either. But if their algorithm stumbles on a design that "goes viral," then Solid Gold Bomb, the T-shirt printer, and Amazon all make money—unless it goes viral for the wrong reasons.

It's a technique that apparently works very well—as of this writing there are 529,493 Solid Gold Bomb clothing items listed for sale on Amazon. Which is not to say that Solid Gold Bomb benefited from trying to sell a T-shirt endorsing rape. In all likelihood, they'll now have to go to the trouble of registering their company under another operating name before resuming business. But it does point to two fundamental problems in how our new technologies work: One, human beings for the most part don't understand the models of production companies currently use; and two, those models are prone to some truly stellar fuck-ups—such as endorsing rape.[3]

Pricing models on Amazon are simple enough to work with, but the problem is severely exacerbated when the system it's attempting to model is more complex. As a slightly more complicated model, look at Google's attempt to predict how big the flu would be the winter of 2012. The idea was that they could analyze where people were when they made flu-related searches on Google, incorporating a bunch of other data about the disease with some rather fancy algorithms to estimate how many people had influenza.

With all the capability of one of the most powerful computing corporations in the world, Google estimated that nearly 11 percent of the United States had influenza at the flu season's peak in mid-January. Which is interesting, especially because estimates by the Centers for Disease Control and Prevention put the peak of the illness at 6 percent.[4]

Declan Butler wrote in *Nature* magazine that the problem may have been because of "widespread media coverage of this year's severe U.S. flu season." If you add in social media you get a nice mix of self-reinforcing media coverage that helped news about the flu to spread quicker—statistically—than the virus itself.[5]

The problem is pretty straightforward. Google knows how to analyze the data it has about people's online behavior pretty well for purposes of predicting other online behavior. But it then took that same data and used it to predict real-world incidences—an entirely different context—and the model got completely FUBAR'd.

In this case, the result was that millions of people thought that the flu was a much, much bigger deal than it really was. Sales of hand sanitizer and Kleenex probably spiked as a result, more people may have taken time off work, and the number of self-diagnosed sick surely rose precipitously.

All of which isn't a huge deal when it's about a common seasonal flu. But what if it happened about incidences of bird flu? Or rumors about stock prices? Or gun ownership? In each case, the enormous reputation of Google lends massive credence to an otherwise completely wrong evaluation based on a single computer calculation. That reputation might not survive the fallout, but by then the damage will have been done, financially, economically, or otherwise.

That's not to say that this was some rank amateur mistake. Google tends to make very few of those. Instead it's illustrative of the kind of weaknesses that computer models tend to have, which is to say that when it comes to real life, the overwhelming complexity tends to lead those models to make big mistakes.

COMPLEX MODELS, FULL OF FAIL

Consider the weather. Everyone always wonders why meteorologists can't get the whole rain / no rain thing right, but in fact they're dealing with an enormously complex system of interconnected elements. But what if you took a simplified situation? Instead of dealing with a mishmash of interplaying microclimates, like the middle of a city, what about the middle of the ocean?

Air France Flight 447, an Airbus 330–200 with 228 people on board, crashed off the Brazilian coast on June 1, 2009, in the Atlantic Ocean in an area where the water is 4,000 meters deep. Put another way, it wasn't a spectacularly complex weather environment. Ordinarily, officials would use a concentric circling method to slowly spiral outward from the last-known or best-guess location to find the plane. It's a technique that's been used for centuries, but in this case French officials decided to do better.[6]

That summer, the French Bureau d'Enquetes et d'Analyses (BEA) contracted renowned oceanographers and mathematicians from France, Great Britain, the United States, and Russia to model the likely location of the crash area to determine where the plane was. They based their model on the drift of the bodies and pieces of the wreckage that had been found on June 6, north of the Last Known Position (LKP). The highly complex calculations took into account currents, wind, and waves and were summed up into a limited 2,000 sq. km probable crash area extending 60 km north of the LKP. The entire effort cost more than $30 million. The result of all this hard work was that they searched in the wrong area for almost two years.

The actual site of the wreckage was only 10 km from the LKP. It was found in late March 2011 when the French Marines, who had placed electronic buoys and monitored them for weeks, found that currents in fact behaved unpredictably and changed very often. The modelers had made wrong assumptions, sending would-be rescuers on a wild goose chase. Now keep in mind that these top minds only had to model 2,000 sq. km for a period of five days, using all the detailed mapping and weather information you would expect a major First World government to be able to provide.

Again, they failed because of their assumptions, which, while enormously well educated, researched, and peer reviewed, were also completely wrong.

It's not just in well-funded government projects that weather models get it wrong. Ross McKitrick of the University of Guelph, an expert reviewer for the UN's Intergovernmental Panel on Climate Change, did an examination of a cadre of major studies attempting to verify weather models. What he learned was that almost all of them were complete and utter shit.[7]

For example, a team of hydrologists at the National Technical University of Athens published a pair of studies in 2008 and 2010 comparing long-term (100-year) temperature and precipitation trends in 55 locations around the world to model projections. The models performed terribly at the annual level, but did equally bad even when averaged up to the 30-year scale, which is the level they were supposed to work best at. They didn't do any better at large regional scales, where small mistakes should have averaged out.[8]

Better yet, a 2011 study in the *Journal of Forecasting* took the same data set and compared the model's predictions against a dummy model made by taking the last period's value in each location as the forecast for the next period. It turns out that purely statistical models sometimes did worse than this "random walk" method (but never better than twice as well), and complex climate models did between twice and four times as well. Four times as well as almost completely random isn't anywhere near accurate, by the way—it's just slightly less than random—and this is at the regional level, even on long time scales, which are supposed to be the easiest and most predictable.[9]

If you want an idea of exactly how badly these models are understood, McKitrick explains how he discovered a competing model:

In a 2010 paper, a co-author and I looked at how well an average formed from all 23 climate models used for the 2007

IPCC report did at explaining the spatial pattern of temperature trends on land after 1979, compared with a rival model
that all the experts keep telling me should have no explanatory
power at all: the regional pattern of socioeconomic growth.
Any effects from those factors, I have been told many times, are
removed from the climate data before it is published. And yet
I keep finding the socioeconomic patterns do a very good job
of explaining the patterns of temperature trends over land. In
our 2010 paper we showed that the climate models, averaged
together, do very poorly, while the socioeconomic data does
quite well.[10]

It may be that socioeconomic data is a really great way to predict the weather, in which case the issue with models is more a
matter of choosing the correct tautology to answer your question
than one of modeling at all. However, I prefer the more obvious
conclusion: Modeling is really hard.

HUMAN JUDGMENT PLUS COMPUTER TECHNOLOGY, FULL OF FAIL

Again, causality is infinite. So what about systems that are
abstracted from messy, dirty, wet reality? How about extremely
closely monitored and deeply analyzed systems that are publicly
visible and tightly regulated...like finance?

How about Amaranth Advisors, who attracted $9 billion
worth of assets and then saw their energy trading strategy fail
as it lost over $6 billion on natural gas futures in 2006.[11] Due to
mild winter conditions and a meek hurricane season, and faced
with faulty risk models and weak natural gas prices, petrol prices
did not bounce back to the levels needed to generate profits, and
$5 billion were lost within a single week. After an intensive inves-
tigation by the US Commodity Futures Trading Commission,

Amaranth was charged with the attempted manipulation of natural gas futures prices.[12] So much for "abstracted models."

Or how about one of the most famous hedge fund collapses, of Long-Term Capital Management (LTCM). Founded in 1994 by John Meriwether of Salomon Brothers fame, its principals included two Nobel Prize–winning economists and a bunch of renowned financial services wizards. The fund began trading with more than $1 billion of capital and promised investors an arbitrage strategy that should, theoretically, reduce the risk level to zero.

The strategy worked well from 1994 to 1998, but when the Russian financial markets started shaking up, LTCM bet big that the situation would revert back to normal quickly. The experts at the fund were so sure of it that they used derivatives to take large, unhedged positions in the market, betting with money they didn't actually have.

In August 1998, Russia defaulted on its debt, leaving LTCM holding huge amounts of Russian government bonds. Despite losing hundreds of millions of dollars per day, LTCM's computer models recommended that it hold its positions. When the losses approached $4 billion, the US federal government feared that the imminent collapse of LTCM would spark a larger financial crisis and bailed them out to calm the markets.

See a trend yet? Human judgment figured in, and things went to hell in a hand basket. Another example: In 2000, despite $6 billion in assets, Julian Robertson's Tiger Management failed utterly. A member of hedge fund royalty, Robertson placed big bets on stocks using a strategy based on buying what he thought were the most promising stocks in the markets and short-selling what he viewed as the worst. Even as a noneconomist, I can understand that—buy good things and short bad ones. Seems rational enough.

This strategy collapsed when the IT bubble hit. Robertson shorted overpriced tech stocks that had nothing but inflated price-to-earnings ratios and no sign of profits anywhere. This was at the same time that major investments were made in companies based on the idea they would sell nothing but pet food online, remember? In fact, long-term, Robertson was right on the money.

Unfortunately, the public didn't catch on to that right away, and tech stocks continued to boom. Tiger Management suffered massive losses and Robertson had to get another job. Once again, human beings had stymied even that most fundamental of all models: common sense.

The point here is that no matter how simple and straightforward the model, when you start applying it to real life the implementation itself is subject to human judgment, and that judgment is often pretty faulty. This makes computer models even harder to use. Even if the model is perfect, it's really hard to apply it anywhere without the risk of making some serious mistakes.

Copyright law provides a great example of this human element throwing a wrench in the works. It's pretty clear to the layman that if you stream a copy of *Transformers* to anyone who wants it on the Internet without paying Paramount Pictures for the right to do so, you're indulging in copyright violation, and Paramount has the legal right to seek damages.

Now extend this with the current technologies available. A computer program can examine a video stream and compare it to a library of copyrighted material—say, all the video content owned by Paramount. The rest seems simple: Create a series of programs, "bots," to examine all video streams you can find and see if they contain copyrighted material. If they do, automatically send a copyright-and-takedown notice.

All very neat and tidy, no? Not to mention profitable—copyright holders are so desperate to recoup what they see as vanishing revenue that dozens of technology companies are jostling to provide technical solutions for enforcing copyright across online communities and video streaming sites. Players like Vobile, Attributor, Audible Magic, and Gracenote are thriving despite the fact that US copyright law (as modified by the 1998 Digital Millennium Copyright Act) doesn't require sites hosting user-created content to preemptively check for copyright violations.

The only problem with this whole scheme is it doesn't work. Earlier this year people trying to watch the streamed video of Michelle Obama's hugely lauded speech at the Democratic National Convention got an unusual notice on YouTube saying that it had been blocked on copyright grounds. More recently, the live stream for the Hugo Awards—the sci-fi and fantasy equivalent of the Oscars—was blocked on Ustream only moments before Neil Gaiman's highly anticipated acceptance speech. Ustream's internal service had detected that the awards were showing copyrighted film clips. Their software had no way to know that the Hugo Awards had already secured permission to use them.

That's the first problem—software can follow explicit instructions, but it rarely picks up the phone to chat with someone about their relationship to content. If it sees copyrighted material and is told to automatically file a cease-and-desist (or a copyright claim, or a takedown notice), then that's what it does. Basically, it's a send-a-takedown-notice-first-and-ask-questions-later world; sending a legal threat is cheap and easy to do, and asking questions is expensive, so the ones doing the threatening generally win.

This problem is greatly exacerbated when you plug it into existing systems, such as small companies that automatically claim copyright on whatever they publish—even if it's an excerpt of a public domain work. For example, footage from NASA's *Curiosity* rover landing got blocked on YouTube multiple times because numerous companies—such as Scripps Local News—claimed copyright on the material, despite the video content being in the public domain.

Those claims were incorrect and likely the result of innocent mistakes or automatic copyrighting policies, all of which the take-down bots knew nothing about. But lo! A relatively simple piece of code nonetheless prevented millions of people from accessing information they had every right to (at least for a while).

The interesting bit, of course, is that everyone loses. Michelle Obama, the Hugo Awards, and even NASA all did their due diligence to make sure their content was readily available. But because the code to pursue copyrighted content was easy to produce—and because it's legally easier to threaten lawsuits than to defend against them—content that should be available often isn't, with nobody making any more money for the effort. The costs were actually enormously high—to Mrs. Obama, the Hugo Awards, and NASA—in terms of their reputation for producing useful content, but that was entirely ignored, because we're all currently operating in a strictly financial model of exchange. Michelle Obama had her speech blocked, but the cost of thousands of fans being unable to see it at the moment it mattered most is a very difficult thing to convert to an exact dollar amount. Everyone knows it was expensive to her reputation. It's just that by cleaving to the fiction that reputation economics don't exist, the copyright bots get to claim that they had no significant impact...or at least not enough impact to be sued over.

THE CALIBRATION CONUNDRUM

Clearly, the erratic human element can create faulty models. It also turns out that models themselves can be intrinsically faulty. For example, in one case, scientist Jonathan Carter wanted to observe what happens to models when they're slightly incorrect, such as when they don't get the physics absolutely right.[13] I recognize that sounds like most models, but bear with me. Doing so required having a baseline model that was perfect, so he could compare the "perfect" model with the flawed one. So Carter set up a model that described a hypothetical oil field's conditions. Because the data was all fictional, he could take the physics to be whatever the model said it was. Then he generated three years of data from his perfect model. This data was "perfect" data, or his baseline. So far so good.

Next he had to "calibrate" the model. Almost all models have parameters that have to be adjusted to make it relevant to the specific situation it's describing—the rate of water flowing over a dam, for example, or the current-carrying capacity of a generator circuit. Calibrating a complex model that doesn't have directly measured parameters usually requires using historic data and adjusting the parameters accordingly so that the model would have "predicted" that historical data. Once that is done the model is considered calibrated, and should theoretically predict what will happen going forward.

Carter had initially used arbitrary parameters in his perfect model to generate perfect data, but now, in order to assess his model in a realistic way, he threw those parameters out and used standard calibration techniques to match his perfect model to his perfect data. It was supposed to be a formality—he assumed, reasonably, that the process would simply produce the same parameters that had been used to produce the data in the first place. But it didn't. It turned out that there were many different sets of parameters that seemed to fit the historical data. And that made sense, he realized—given a mathematical expression with many terms and parameters in it, and thus many different ways to add up to the same single result, you'd expect there to be different ways to tweak the parameters so they can produce similar sets of data over some limited time period.

The problem, of course, is that while these different versions of the model might all match the historical data, they would generate different predictions going forward. And sure enough, his calibrated model produced terrible predictions compared to the "reality" originally generated by the perfect model. Calibration—a standard procedure used by all modelers in all fields, including finance—had rendered a perfect model seriously flawed. Though taken aback, he continued his study and found that having even tiny flaws in the model or the historical data made the situation far worse. "As far as I can tell, you'd have exactly the same situation with any model that has to be calibrated," says Carter.[14]

If you want a complex model that will reflect reality, you need to calibrate it. And if you calibrate it, it's more likely to be wrong, especially if you use historic data. To understand why this impacts reputation exchanges, imagine how stunningly inaccurate your Klout score, or any other general metric of popularity or influence using your online social record, must be over time. Weighing your number of followers on Twitter against the use of expletives by friends of friends on Facebook against how many times per week someone who claims to be an executive views your LinkedIn account is tricky business. Now take all those different contexts and make some maths to reliably represent your ability to influence someone—anyone—on any platform about any topic in any context. Oh, and make sure those maths result in a single number anyone can apply anywhere.

That's hard enough, but let's just say it could be done. Voilà! You have a single number that works. So what happens tomorrow? Or the day after? Or once you get married, or have a kid, or discover religion, or get addicted to prescription drugs, or take a new job, or start getting into brewing your own kombucha? You need to recalibrate, because your context, behavior, relationships, content, and more have suddenly changed. It's an ongoing problem, and despite the incredibly advanced technology designed to make sense out of all that change—and adapt to it—the problem doesn't become less complicated because of it.

Klout is perhaps the best example of why this is an issue because it's fundamentally based on an extraordinarily multicontextualized set of data—your reputation. The human brain is really good at reconciling and recalibrating its own model of human behavior (although it's not perfect by any means) over time. If you made a bunch of off-color jokes last month on Facebook but I know you were dating that one hot mess from out of town, I'm liable to forgive it, but that's a pretty specific set of criteria to represent in a mathematical model. Computer models simply aren't there yet, and even if they were able to pull it off in multiple instances, they're still subject to the calibration problem explained above.

Which isn't to say they'll be this bad forever; if we've proven anything as a species it's our ability to iterate our technologies into something more effective. Note that *effective* isn't necessarily *good*, however. As much as I'm sure we'll see versions of Klout that work better (probably by being more domain specific), it's unlikely we'll see one that works really well across a wide variety of domains. That's due to what I call the multiple experts effect.

THE MULTIPLE EXPERTS EFFECT

Models get even more complicated once you start adding additional experts from different fields, which is a must if you want to model something that affects more than one field (and what, realistically, doesn't?). For example, take a 107-page paper by Oded Galor of Brown University in Providence, Rhode Island, and Quamrul Ashraf of Williams College in Williamstown, Massachusetts. The paper has been peer reviewed by economists and biologists, and as of this printing is slated to appear in one of the most prestigious economics journals, the *American Economic Review*.

The paper argues that there are strong links between estimates of genetic diversity for 145 countries and per capita incomes, even after accounting for myriad factors such as economic-based migration.[15] Basically, it states that the higher the diversity, the greater the innovation potential. The paper was very popular among economists for over two years, until *Science* published a summary in its section on new research in other journals. The resulting shitstorm included responses from a strikingly long list of prominent scientists, including geneticist David Reich of Harvard Medical School and Harvard University paleoanthropologist Daniel Lieberman.

In an open letter, they said they were worried that "the suggestion that an ideal level of genetic variation could foster economic growth and could even be engineered has the potential to be misused with frightening consequences to justify indefensible practices such as ethnic cleansing or genocide."[16] In this case the error had nothing to do with the model; it was simply impolitic for another group of scientists. This sort of nuanced political difference is nearly impossible for an algorithm to recognize and adapt to, especially dynamically, and yet those same algorithms are being used to create platforms of exchange around the world. It reminds of the Chevy Nova, whose name apparently tested well in focus groups before being shipped to Mexico, where it was discovered that "Nova" means "it doesn't go" in Spanish.

That's exactly the kind of error computer systems are liable to make around reputation-dependent issues and is another big part of why reputation is so noncomputational.

FAULTY CONCLUSIONS AND THE ENUMERATION OF HR

All of which is OK—models have traditionally just been guideposts we've used to aid intuition and expert opinion. But now we're making machines that act intelligently based on them, such as the previously mentioned example of Xerox hiring 3,500 new jobs based on models. In this case, Xerox did surveys of hires who worked in their call centers who stuck around long enough for Xerox to get their $5,000 worth of training (which they'd invested in each new hire) back through a long-enough period of being a satisfactory employee. They also compared the survey results of employees who didn't. Then, through a little math, a little modeling, and a few layoffs in HR, they replaced their hiring process (which was done by people) *with the survey itself.*[17]

They'd discovered that they had enough "good" results from employees who stayed and enough "bad" results from employees who didn't that they could compare the survey from a potential new employee and grade how deeply it fell into one category or the other. Turn the survey into a web form that applicants can fill out remotely, and employee attrition was cut by one-fifth.

This isn't really that surprising. As a baseline test, it probably does a pretty good job. But the devil is in the details, as they say, and in this case I have to wonder what the long-term effect of hiring based on algorithm will reveal. For example, the survey may be worded in such a way that applicants who aren't into baseball may misunderstand some of the examples, and therefore be hired less often. Or it may trend toward men versus women, or young people versus older folks. Any of these factors might emerge as being ignored by the survey, with some large-scale potential problems for Xerox's hiring practices vis-à-vis the state—we won't know until Xerox has hired a large enough group of people, enough so that the problems become starkly visible.

Even more implausible is hiring by Klout score. And yet that's also happening increasingly often.

Klout.com is an online "reputation score" system, which takes all your social software accounts—your Twitter, Facebook, LinkedIn, and other accounts—and does some algorithmic magic to determine your "influence." What is this algorithm? What does it take into account? What is it measuring, and why, and with what parameters? Nobody knows except Klout. And yet like some modern-day Friendster, everybody is suddenly rushing to make their magic Klout score rise above their peers'.

This would be amusing except that it is *actually happening.* Imagine if your ability to get employed as a tax collector was dependent on the number of Twitter followers who had "liked" your tweets. If you're not popular enough (based on a largely arbitrary and potentially irrelevant metric), you don't get the job. Simple . . . and stupid.

As Seth Stevenson wrote in an article in *Wired*:

Last spring Sam Fiorella was recruited for a VP position at a large Toronto marketing agency. With 15 years of experience consulting for major brands like AOL, Ford, and Kraft, Fiorella felt confident in his qualifications. But midway through the interview, he was caught off guard when his interviewer asked him for his Klout score. Fiorella hesitated awkwardly before confessing that he had no idea what a Klout score was.

The interviewer pulled up the web page for Klout.com—a service that purports to measure users' online influence on a scale from 1 to 100—and angled the monitor so that Fiorella could see the humbling result for himself: His score was 34. "He cut the interview short pretty soon after that," Fiorella says. Later he learned that he'd been eliminated as a candidate specifically because his Klout score was too low. "They hired a guy whose score was 67."[18]

Fiorella was curious—and scared—by the experience and took the next 6 months to raise his Klout score, getting up to 72. As that number rose, so did the number of speaking invitations and job offers he got. "Fifteen years of accomplishments weren't as important as that score," he said.[19]

Keep in mind that the only "perfect 100" score on Klout belongs to Justin Bieber, whereas President Obama's score is currently at 91. One would think we'd pause before glorifying a metric that ranks a teen pop star as more influential than the leader of the free world, in which case one would be wrong. Mostly that's because the *concept* of a metric that ranks social influence in one, easy-to-monitor number is so damn appealing. Human beings are hardwired to compete, and simple numerical representations are potent triggers for that little endorphin rush we get when our number goes up. It's a fundamental principle in game design (games being simplified models of competition), and it works very much in Klout's favor. But it's not by any means an indication that Klout actually models social influence in any useful way. As a friend of mine remarked, it's like giving a free hotel room upgrade to someone who is popular for trashing hotel rooms—which is happening increasingly often as hotels look for ways to amortize marketing costs by comping rooms to patrons with "influence."

None of this makes Klout any less convenient or conventional for use in choosing whether to hire someone, or give them a discount, or to accept them as a friend. It completely ignores the fact that slamming a product is a great way to generate followers on Twitter, making some very popular tweeters into really bad candidates for investment by brands, or ignores that your Klout score can get you free entrance to your airline's first class lounge just by buying fake twitter accounts until your score is high enough. In both cases the design of the system results in behavior directly counter to the goals of its clients.

In this way Klout may be slowly racking up secondary- and tertiary-level negative effects we won't see until it collapses. That collapse could be sudden, a la Friendster, or slower, a la the US real estate market. Either way, it won't be pretty as it dawns on us all that Klout doesn't actually represent influence. It just models it, in one particular, narrow, and—for now—relatively unique way.

Personally, I'm not so concerned about reputation metrics like Klout. Perhaps I'm being overly optimistic, but I choose to believe that the average person realizes that posting 40 or more times a day (which is currently necessary to keep up a respectable Klout score) isn't necessarily representative of their ability to prepare tax forms well. Instead, I'm more concerned about the confluence of all this technological capability, and what starts to bleed when its cutting edge slides against the gnarly, uninspected preconceptions of the models we're predicating its use on.

GHOST TRADERS

In early October 2012 a single trader began placing orders in 25-millisecond bursts for roughly 500 stocks, according to Nanex, a market data firm. Eric Hunsader, head of Nanex (the no. 1 detector of trading anomalies watching Wall Street today), picked up that this was a single high-frequency trader algorithm after seeing a pattern in the trades—200 fake quotes, then 400, then 1,000, repeated ad infinitum. That algorithm never *executed* a single trade—only placed them—and ended abruptly at about 10:30 a.m. EST that Friday.[20]

The interesting part of these "mystery algorithms" is that the prevailing theory is that they're garbage designed to slow down the network. According to Nanex, this one particular trader's millions of quotes accounted for 10 percent of the bandwidth allowed for trading on any given day. By making other traders' orders take effect ever so slightly more slowly than the algorithm's owner, they give him or her an edge in placing *real* orders. But it's also been

hypothesized that the algorithm is designed to probe certain traders or networks for responsiveness in preparation for an organized
attack—again, to allow a map of order delivery speeds across the
network so automated trades can be designed in which the seller
or buyer knows in advance if he/she will be able to have them
placed before the competition.

Either way, this "garbage" trading could become a serious
problem very quickly. The market is predicated on the idea that
everyone has equal access to making trades—there are no controls
to keep one trader from being faster than another because his/her
algorithm has a faster network connection to a particular buyer.
The model isn't designed to take into account trade latency due
to network topology. And yet, obviously, algorithmically assisted
trades *do* provide an advantage. Consider that high-frequency trading (read: algorithmically generated) accounts for up to 70 percent
of *all* trading activity each day. So what happens if one of them
gets a *big* lead on the others? Aside from complete disruption of the
financial markets, potentially leading to the abandonment of the
NASDAC and the related collapse of the US economy, I mean?

Faulty models—either due to flawed design or lack of fore-
sight—are dangerous. They're exploitable, sure, but they're also
dangerous in and of themselves, because they fall down in ways we
don't expect. After all, if we *did* expect them to fail in a certain way,
we'd be prepared for the results and take steps to prevent them. As
ever, it's what *you don't know* you don't know that hurts you.

BABIES AND BATHWATER

So we know there is more technological capability than ever before,
and we know it's all predicated on some pretty flawed models
that stand to make some cataclysmically bad mistakes. And all
this is happening in an environment where new technologies are

infiltrating more and more deeply into every aspect of our lives in ways most of us cannot comprehend. As that happens, new computer models are being created that will—unwittingly or not—reshape society as we know it, through business, politics, and culture.

This puts us on some pretty thin ice, both as a species and as a society. A global collapse of the stock market is as likely as a cataclysmic failure of the energy grid, and neither is immune to bad political decisions whose impacts are exacerbated by increasingly powerful platforms like Klout.

In many ways the growing power of unified reputation systems is particularly daunting when viewed against the ongoing conflict of simple pieces of code such as those Amazon book reseller bots; the result is clearly an arms race of automated influence ending with the devaluation of whatever reputation measures were being used in the first place. The downside to this is that it simply bankrupts those systems and everyone who used them, which can only set us back from the positive progress we have made with these new technologies.

Friendster.com is a great example of this. Initially a hugely popular site, it saw an amazingly steep adoption curve as everybody created an account to start building up their "Friend" score. The way you did that, of course, was to get more friends, which led more and more people to use less and less meaningful ways to get someone to say they were a friend. In the end people were writing bots to make fake friends, some people were buying lots of friends to boost their score, and nobody knew if someone's high friend score had anything at all to do with their actual number of friends anymore. Your "friend" score became meaningless, the system bankrupted itself, and everyone gave up on Friendster.

In some ways that's simply the instinct of the system. Scarcity-oriented, closed systems aren't designed to expand value beyond their borders. It's similar to how Facebook's personal data analysis is different from how you look at people on the street. Facebook is trying to make very discreet judgments about you that they can turn into money. When you're walking down the street and see someone new, you have a multitude of goals in mind, and so you make many assessments that vary by how you're feeling at the moment but that also can be revised in hindsight. If you see someone wearing an outfit you despise, but they suddenly stop and help an old lady who just fell down, it's pretty easy to find yourself being forgiving of their sartorial ambitions. Financially driven computer systems don't enjoy that same flexibility.

So where does that leave us? Are we doomed to destruction by bad tweeting? Or is there a harmonious possible future wherein computer-aided human intuition can guide us? Is there a way our faulty models can avoid systemic collapse by relying on the human brain's ability to synthesize fuzzy data sets of cross-tautological expertise and synchronous, evolutionary inputs? Thankfully, yes.

MINSKY VS. LEARY

Part of the answer, I think, lies in an age-old split in the computer science community. I'm putting my head on the block here—this argument has raged for years, making and breaking careers, and as our capabilities in computer technology have increased so has its fervor. No matter what I say, some will be offended, but I think it's worth at least outlining the argument in order to suggest one way forward with the technology we're developing today. I'm speaking, of course, about Artificial Intelligence (AI) versus Intelligence Augmentation (IA).

Artificial intelligence, or "Strong AI," is explained by noted futurist Ray Kurzweil as "artificial intelligence that matches or exceeds human intelligence—the intelligence of a machine that can successfully perform any intellectual task that a human being can."[21] Wikipedia explains it thusly: "Strong AI is also referred to as 'artificial general intelligence' or as the ability to perform 'general intelligent action.' Strong AI is associated with traits such as consciousness, sentience, sapience and self-awareness observed in living beings."[22]

Again, I'm summarizing thousands of papers and books, and hundreds to thousands of hours of debate and blood-sweat-and-tears into a couple of paragraphs here, so bear with me if the summary seems unconventionally brief. For the purposes of my argument, suffice to say that the idea behind Strong AI is to re-create many of the core competencies of the human mind.

Intelligence Augmentation, on the other hand, is "the effective use of information technology in augmenting human intelligence."[23] One could say we've been doing this since the abacus and even before, but you get the idea. Basically, this is taking what we already have and making it function better—more efficiently, faster, and more accurately—and is essentially what most information technology developed up to the modern day is aimed at.

While these ideas clearly overlap and diverge in a variety of ways, both have as their goal (ostensibly) the advancement and empowerment of the human race. But it's the essential differences that I think point us to a way forward with the tools we have in front of us now.

One way to think about it is as Marvin Minsky versus Timothy Leary. Marvin Minsky is an American cognitive scientist who cofounded MIT's AI laboratory and has authored some of the most seminal works on AI, AI theory, and AI practice. He invented a number of groundbreaking technologies, including one of the first head-mounted displays, and has won numerous awards in a variety of areas. In short, he's a consummate scientist and one of the leaders in his field.

Timothy Leary, on the other hand, was an American psychologist and writer best known for his advocacy of psychedelic drugs. Famously, President Richard Nixon described Leary as "the most dangerous man in America." He encouraged recreational drug use; helped found several spiritual groups; was a huge advocate of space travel, life extension, and other theories; was convicted of numerous crimes; and was an enormous figure in popular counterculture.

One could say they shared equally insurmountable goals—be that a space ark filled with 5,000 virile compatriots or creating a computer system that can think like a human being—but their approaches were vastly different.

The reason I highlight Leary as a counterpoint to Minsky is that Leary was dedicated to creating change through leveraging the human mind in a multitude of ways—meditation, marijuana, alternative culture, and cognitive therapy—whereas Minsky wanted simply to reduce and re-create it in silicon. That's effectively what we're seeing happen with technology development today, especially when it comes to reputation systems. To turn something into code, after all—to codify—means to "arrange according to a plan or system."[24] Compare that to the concept of leveraging what already exists and iterating the results, which entails having more open-ended results.

I'm as guilty of hubris as anyone, and even I'm taken aback by the idea that we can imagine—and replicate—the plan behind the human mind. Not that it's impossible, but the effort is staggering in scope. AI is a critical and important branch of computer science research, and Minsky has my backing for it every time. But for the problems of this decade, this year, of today, I'm going with Leary and trying more methods more frequently. Doing so allows us to put more of an emphasis on results we can measure this year, whether those results are failures we can use to iterate our designs past or successes to build on. If nothing else, building fast and releasing often will help us understand the multitudes of ways in which all these new technologies *can* be applied, and give us a leg up on creating the 20 percent of the solution that can answer 80 percent of the problem.

So what does that mean for the panopticon and all that crazy capability floating around on the Internet right now? It's actually really simple.

AUGMENT...PEOPLE

Reputation economies are extremely human endeavors, created through a long process of adaptation and evolution from which we've become very adept as a species, and are how most commerce has happened to date. What we're seeing happen with our technology now is often an attempt to replace or replicate—at scale—these systems, especially with the goal of repurposing them to extract maximum financial return. This is quite different from attempting to augment—through any and all means available—the inherently human capabilities we already have within us.

When Brand X hosts a marketing campaign run by bots pretending to be friends of your friends to encourage you to "friend" their Facebook page, they aren't actually becoming your friend in return. While Brand X may eventually give you a candy bar or tote bag, the cost/benefit equation is fraught with externalities that only the human being can pay, namely time, attention, and the resultant ennui. Again, this is an attempt to re-create, computationally, one of the mechanisms of an extraordinarily complex and dyadic gift economy known as "friendship"; it is a means to convince you to spend some time and effort pretending to have a meaningful relationship to a snippet of code in front of other real people whom that code would like to impress.

By way of contrast, Skillshare.com isn't replacing the process of learning to paint by having someone show you how. Instead, it's taking the completely intuitive social method of finding someone who knows how to paint and connecting you. It isn't as great a technological achievement as replicating the human mind digitally, such as AI proposes, but it's also a goal that has actually been achieved, today. The distinction is important.

What I'm suggesting is that by relying heavily on models that are supposed to be all-inclusive and correct, we're leaving a lot of capability on the table—specifically, we're leaving human beings out of the mix. For one thing, our biases in making these models is inextricably linked to how human minds see the world. Trying to scrub those biases rather than considering them as part of the model from the start adds a blind spot that's terrifically difficult to get around. For another, our own brains are *awesome* machines. By leveraging our own capabilities through IA rather than by trying to cut ourselves out of the loop, we're able, often, to produce better results.

Amazon's Mechanical Turk is a great example. The service allows you to make microtasks which you then pay a very small amount of money to have someone perform. The idea is that human beings are uniquely capable in ways that machines simply cannot match, and that a simple platform to allow you to hire people to do these tasks is a good way to utilize that. The scope of what this kind of system can do is immense; by way of example, take Jim Gray.

On January 28, 2007, Gray, a well-known researcher and manager of Microsoft Research's eScience Group, sailed out under the Golden Gate Bridge headed for the Farallon Islands, where he was going to scatter his mother's ashes. He never returned. The Coast Guard searched 132,000 square miles of ocean and found nothing. What happened next was extraordinary.

Meanwhile, Gray's friends, a well-connected and redoubtable bunch, organized. They got NASA to fly a reconnaissance plane over the area and take photos. They got the Canadian Space Agency to re-direct its radar satellite; they got both Microsoft and Microsoft's mortal enemy, Google, to re-direct their satellites. All that imagery needed to be sorted through for a tiny boat in a sea of gray pixels. Computers aren't much good at that, so Gray's friends got Amazon to upload those images into a website it ran called the Mechanical Turk, on which companies paid people to do jobs that only human intelligence could. Mechanical Turk's 12,000 volunteers flipped through over 560,000 images, covering almost 3,500 square miles of ocean. Then a cohort of oceanographers, computer scientists, and astronomers ran simulations of where ocean currents might have taken the boat and compared the different satellites' images and re-processed those images. And because astronomers have eyes and brains trained to pick out tiny visual signals from noise, the astronomers flipped through the images as well."[25]

Jim Gray was never found, which is a terrible loss. But the power of Mechanical Turk was demonstrated in a stunning example of how to combine the best capabilities of the human mind with the scope and scale of the Internet.

In addition to the kind of software design that emphasizes enhancing human capabilities, I would posit that we can make greater strides by harnessing a multitude of different sociological, cultural, and technological approaches to reputation economies than we will by attempting to use our newfound computational power to force extant models of financial exchange on top of them. This isn't to say that technology is a poor tool for reputation exchanges—quite the opposite. Rather, it's an enormously powerful one that we're hobbling with our limited view of its application. Much as Leary suggested we expand our minds through a panoply of means—whether as banal as exercise or as obtuse as alien mindsex—I would suggest that by trying many new things with tech (like building software designed to utilize key human strengths instead of replacing them), we'll find better applications for it than if we simply copy what we think has been done before.

CHAPTER 7
THE ABUNDANCE ECONOMY

A NEW TWIST ON AN OLD THEME

In fact, we're already trying newer things with our technology than simply copying past efforts. One of the most significant ways in which this is happening is in using technology to reshape commerce from fiat-currency-based (scarcity) to reputation-based (abundance) economies. In the effort to make our existing systems more efficient, we've created a bevy of technologies and commercial platforms that are reshaping how commerce is done. It's completely organic and unplanned, but the emergent effects are starting to shape up to look awfully familiar.

Historically, scarcity ruled our markets. There was only so much grain available in a given field, only so many fish in the river, only so many rugs woven in a season. But the way we *exchanged* those goods was often oriented around maximizing their reach: through gift economies or trade emphasizing mutual benefit. Frequently, a limited amount of a particular good was still able to create more value than the sum of its parts.

For the first time, we're starting to see that same effect happen again. Except this time, it's because the grain, the fish, and the rugs are becoming virtual. Infinitely reproducible, freely and limitlessly distributable. For the first time, the idea of a thing—its design—is enabling us to maximize our return, and to do it in a way that more people benefit from. It's a new economy—one of abundance.

THE THINGIVERSE AND 3D PRINTING

When I say "abundance economy" I don't mean to infer that the planet has become richer than before. Aside from the occasional meteorite we have the same materials to work with that we always have—and nowadays we have a lot more people to use them up. Instead, I'm referring to both physical and virtual goods. And in terms of the physical, the biggest change is in hyperlocalized, on-demand physical production and globally distributed designs.

There's a trend in Brooklyn, New York, where families are buying MakerBots—breadmaker-sized boxes you assemble yourself that use extruded plastic to "print" 3D objects. Why families? Because small, complicated, and unique plastic parts make up 75 percent of the expensive-to-replace components that break on strollers and children's toys.

The value in these pieces isn't in the plastic that comprises them—a few cents of plastic is a few cents of plastic anywhere in the world. But the specific design required is worth quite a bit, and until now that design was owned by the stroller manufacturer, who would often require you buy a whole new stroller to replace it.

Now, however, you can log onto Thingiverse.com—a community-run meritocracy of people who make 3D designs for printing on machines like the MakerBot—and download exactly what you need, usually for free. A few cents of generic plastic thread in your Makerbot, and your stroller is up and running again. Right now there are more than 32,000 discrete designs on Thingiverse. When I spoke to Bre Pettis, one of the founders, over 6,000 had been uploaded in the last 90 days alone. It's growing fast, and it's hugely popular for anyone who has access to a 3D printer.

Keep in mind that as of this book's printing, we're on the fourth generation of the Makerbot, with significantly better resolution, and the wizards at MakerBot Labs are currently working on printing 3D objects with multiple materials. That means you might be able to "print" a fully functional computer, cell phone, or other device in the near future.[1] For that matter, serious investors are already sinking cash into companies looking to 3D print meat and other foods.[2] And while it's not exactly an endorsement, you can already find, download, and print a fully functional firearm.[3] In the Netherlands, there's an architecture firm that's in the process of printing an entire *house*.[4]

This shift moves design to the forefront of product development—ahead of manufacture, distribution, or anything else. Design as the most significant requirement of a product is an interesting twist, as it's completely nonphysical, and as we've noted, nonphysical goods are extraordinarily native to the way commerce has evolved on the Internet.

As a good example, look at how disrupted the music and movie industries were when their products went from being physical goods—CDs or DVDs—to being nonphysical goods—MP3 or AVI files. All of a sudden the markets for these goods shifted completely, moving from the physical, brick-and-mortar method of selling, shopping, and buying movies and music to an online model. Pricing changed. Distribution changed. Advertising changed. All because the good was now nonphysical, meaning infinitely reproducible, (nearly) freely distributable, and completely derivable.

Those features are all now true of most anything in your home as we approach being able to "print" most physical goods. Like a chair you saw in a store? Now you can snap a picture (or series of pictures) of it, import those photos into a computer program, and use it to derive a 3D model that you can then tweak, color, size, and then print in a variety of materials. Or you can just ask a web-based platform to try to recognize the chair in the photo and recommend the nearest match from an open-source library of similar chairs—all of which you can also tweak, color, size, and then print, laser cut, etch, and have delivered.

In other words, all the ancillary costs that previously limited the production of a physical good—shipping, manufacture, advertising, distribution, sales, and more—are now enormously attenuated. Instead, the primary cost of any individual obtaining that new chair is in its design. Once the design exists, it can be edited by anyone, printed anywhere, and distributed across a plethora of platforms for free.

That's a big difference from the primarily scarce resources that underpinned the production of most goods so far in human history. Now, with the abundance economy, the design of the chair is the most valuable attribute of the chair itself. Sure, I'll pay or trade or friend or follow you if you turn me on to a steady stream of cool things that include chairs (curating), and/or I may pay a premium to have you print my chair instead of printing it myself (production), and of course I'm happy to exchange more value to have it sent to my house preassembled (distribution), but none of those things holds a candle to the value of the initial act of creating the chair in the first place. If you can do that—design chairs that people really want—and do it reliably, you now hold the keys to the real value of those chairs.

That's because the more I am known as someone who designs badass chairs, the more people will want my designs and the more I can charge for them before they even exist, be that through barter, trade, or finance. Case in point is PrettySmallThings, aka Casey Holgrin. By day she's a set designer for Broadway shows, in which she practices the old method of financial exchange. The director explains a set design he wants, and she goes and creates a single design that she then delivers to him in exchange for financial compensation for her time and effort. It's a pretty standard arrangement.[5]

Except that a couple years ago she started using a Makerbot 3D printer to create the pieces of her designs. Previously, she would have to use exacto knives and cardboard and glue and wax to create a set of tiny Elizabethan chairs, for example. Now, she designs enormously detailed Elizabethan chairs and prints them. That's pretty cool, and certainly makes her day job more efficient. After all, if she needs six chairs, she can just design and print one six times.

But there's a side effect to this. She then takes those designs and puts them on Thingiverse under a Creative Commons license that only requires that you provide attribution (give credit to Holgrin) for the design—it's otherwise "free" to download, remix, and distribute. Now, anyone in the world who wants to print out an Elizabethan chair can just download her designs and print them, or pay her a fee and have her print them and ship them.

Completely outside of the revenue of printing and shipping her designs (which I don't think is her main interest), PrettySmallThings is benefiting terrifically from this arrangement. For a start, she's getting pretty well known for her work, meaning that if she wanted to do something else related to design, she now has a hell of a reputation to work with. This also means she can ask for more in exchange for doing this work, since she's got a widespread audience of people who have downloaded and loved her designs and who are willing to vouch for her. And finally, she's got a load of people who are eager to work with her or have her design things, all of which are raising the value of her time. In other words, by giving away her designs "for free," she's accumulating loads of other kinds of value, all of which can result not just in direct trades for things she wants, but can also create opportunities to do or get things she didn't know she wanted. That's an abundance economy—by giving something away, everyone gets more than they would have otherwise.

ROBOTIC AUTOMATION

At the same time that people are increasingly able to make things at home, things that need to be made elsewhere are being made more cheaply—by robots. The advent of low-cost automation fore-tells changes on the scale of the revolution in agricultural technology over the last century, when farming employment in the United States fell from 40 percent of the work force to about 2 percent today.[6]

The same advances in machine vision, computer intelligence, and sensor technologies that allow so much information to be collected about people are now being built into robots, meaning that they are able to replace more and more of what were previously human-only jobs, leading to even more hyperlocalization of production. Concomitant to that are a reduction in the costs of distribution and manufacture and an increase in the value of design.

As one example, at Earthbound Farms in California, four robot arms with suction-cup attachments pick and place organic lettuce containers into boxes for shipping. The robots move much faster than the people they replaced—and each robot replaces between two and five workers at Earthbound. This is according to John Dulchinos, chief executive at robot maker Adept Technology, which developed Earthbound's system.[7]

This replacement is primarily a function of cost. Last year in Chicago at a car show, director of robotics technology Ron Potter, of Atlanta consulting firm Factory Automation Systems, showed attendees a spreadsheet calculating how fast robots would pay for themselves. In one case, a robotic manufacturing system cost $250,000. While that's definitely a big up-front cost, that robot replaced two machine operators who would have cost the company $100,000 that year ($50,000 each in salary). Over an estimated 15-year system lifetime, the machines produced $3.5 million in savings—and never called in sick.

As these machines get more and more capable, they're becoming more and more common. Recently, Hyundai and Beijing Motors completed a massive factory outside Beijing that can make a million vehicles a year—using robots. It also uses far fewer people than the big factories of their competitors, said Paul Chau, an American venture capitalist at WI Harper who toured the plant.[8]

This cost in jobs for human beings is endemic, for all the same reasons we use tractors powered by diesel instead of horses and calculate spreadsheets on computers instead of with an abacus. But the impact is difficult to overstate. In one case, a warehouse for Kroger grocery stores installed a German system that automatically stores and retrieves cases of food, leading to the elimination of 106 jobs—roughly 20 percent of the existing work force. While the new system was maintained initially by senior union workers, the job eventually went to the German company who hired (cheaper) nonunion workers.[9]

That sort of scaling up of robot labor is going to continue to increase, meaning that things you cannot make at home can be made more cheaply, and made closer to wherever the consumer is. Incidentally, the two technologies are convergent; 3D printing in your home uses many similar technologies to the robots staffing production lines in plants in China. That means that smaller, more nimble, more localized plants can eventually be built to satisfy demand without the need for so many centralized resources and the large costs of shipping finished goods between them.

THE DECENTRALIZATION OF SHOPPING

Now link this with Amazon's recent move toward paying sales tax. They resisted doing this for years, for obvious reasons, but recently agreed to start doing it in six more states. Why? One very popular theory is that they've finally realized that the value proposition for Amazon.com isn't selling Amazon-branded goods (like books) for cheaper. It's selling whatever people want *more conveniently*. For years retailers thought that shopping online would never be perceived as superior to buying in a store because you cannot actually handle the goods you're considering buying. But it turns out that all this online validation (backed by reputation) is turning that into a moot argument.

Sure, most people still want to try on a pair of jeans to see how their butt looks before they buy it, but do you have to do that to buy a new camera? Or a spatula? No—instead, you compare the numerous votes for or against it, weigh the reviews you want to read, and then hit "buy." Given the enormous amount of options available to you, whether online or in a physical store, weighting by reviews is actually *easier* than comparing all the options yourself.

After that, the added effort of having to then get in a car and go somewhere to pick the damn thing up is of no added value, meaning that all of a sudden having something delivered to your home is a huge savings. That's changed Amazon's value proposition significantly, and it means that they're starting to build smaller, localized warehouses so they can ship more things, faster (optimally overnight). The additional number of customers they'll convert by being able to offer all that intelligence about their products (again, reputational assessment of their goods, meaning buyers are more confident in what they buy) and their customers (massive data tracking of who buys what when and what to offer as an upsell) is more than worth the added cost in taxes, which the states have been pressuring them mercilessly about for years now anyway. In simpler terms, their ability to get you what you want faster means they'll move more product, making up for the increased cost in taxes they'll have to pay in exchange for having a business presence (i.e., a warehouse) in more states.

All of which is good for the consumer. With less costs associated with storing goods in warehouses (when you can print them out on an as-needed basis instead), greater confidence in purchasing decisions due to widespread reputation assessments through reviews or quantitative purchasing analysis, and cheaper production and shipping costs due to robots, the overall price of most consumer goods should only go down—all while the value of the design (which has the most impact on a good's quality) goes up.

Ironically, this same shift can also be unexpectedly good for employment. As robots and 3D printers become cheaper, "reshoring"—the opposite of "offshoring"—is happening more and more. The need for educated operators of this high-tech equipment is the same, but now they're needed where that equipment is, which is increasingly local (near the markets they want to ship to) instead of millions of miles away in cheaper manufacturing economies like China. There are less jobs overall as robots and new manufacturing techniques replace blue-collar labor, but in exchange the jobs that *are* available are increasingly coming home as manufacturing becomes more distributed. Along the way, the renewed emphasis on design means that more and more opportunities exist for designers to create, market, and sell their products independently, meaning a bigger market for a different class of knowledge work. I'm not promising a utopian boom of work to counter all unemployment, but hopefully it's a small swing in the right direction.

FREE IS BETTER THAN (ARTIFICIALLY) SCARCE

Before we get deeper into this primacy of design, let's step aside for a moment and talk about some of the smoking wrecks on the side of the information superhighway, most notably the previous incarnations of the music and movie businesses. As much as they're popular firestarters in the ongoing argument about Intellectual Property, they're also excellent examples of how big business can miss the boat in handling a changing market. Both were predicated on the idea that information could only be exchanged by physically handing you a physical artifact that had the data stored on it. In large part, that was the case for most of human history—since Gutenberg's time, large-scale data transmission was generally limited to stacks of thinly pressed wood or skins.

This limitation echoes the problems commerce has always had up until very recently. Because the scale at which data could be shared was limited to those people you could reach out and touch, efficient means of distribution were at a premium and required copious intermediaries to facilitate the transaction. That's why it made sense (supposedly) to charge $12 for 5 cents worth of plastic with 11 songs you didn't want and one song you did want etched on it.

But then the Internet came along, and the human race discovered what it had known *before* these limitations of scale appeared. Before we knew there was another village in the next valley, we freely exchanged information with everyone around us with the expectation that we wouldn't lose the information in the process. A song, once sung, couldn't be taken back out of the ears of the listener. The only way to derive value from a limitless good like data was through means of exchange such as a gift economy—through increasing abundance, rather than scarcity. Singing your song to many people, and having them sing it to many other people, extended the value via building your reputation.

That's what the Internet did to the movie and music industries: It reminded us all that bits (information) can only endure temporary scarcity through artificial limitation, and that once they're shared they no longer suffer those limitations. Just because some bits are encoded in a way that computers can read and most people can't doesn't erase the fundamental concept of information as free. And so people learned to decode the music their computers heard so they could share them, and found better and more efficient ways to share them, turning the scarcity economy of movies and music (DVDs and CDs) into an abundance economy (MP3s and AVIs and other formats.)

The result has been a huge increase in the money made by the movie industry, despite its absolute best efforts to stuff the genie back into the bottle. In 2012, for the first time in history, total ticket sales exceeded $10.7 billion, with 2013 revenue estimated to reach $10.8 billion. Note that this record was reached *without raising ticket prices*.[10] At the same time, the total number of movies premiered in 2012 also went up to a record-breaking 655 movies released. Internationally, box office revenues have been growing consecutively for several years—international grosses nearly tripled over the past decade from $8.1 billion in 2001 to $22.4 billion in 2011.[11] This is all apparently due to the increased exposure these movies are getting by being freely shared, resulting in an increased appetite for a premium experience (such as seeing the film in a movie theater).

Music is starting to see the same effect, with subscription music services experiencing a revenue increase of 13.5 percent in 2011 (from $212 to $241 million), with paying customers climbing 18 percent (from 1.5 to 1.8 million), according to the RIAA.[12]

The Internet hasn't dissolved the value of music or movies; it's simply removed the artificial costs of all the middlemen that used to be required for distribution. That means that the people who are producing the goods, and those who are consuming them, are all able to benefit directly, because now when I want to check out an artist or preview a movie, I can do so for free, instantly, via the Internet.

That's what happened to an entrenched, thoroughly physical-goods–oriented business ecology. Now imagine what will evolve in its stead as *other* types of data emerge. We know that what happened to movies and music is also changing e-books, magazines, newspapers, and other forms of media, but what about goods that don't exist yet? What happens when 3D printers start being able to make food or medicine? What is going to emerge as E-Ink picture frames are able to display any piece of artwork ever made? Or car designs begin to make use of the gigantic third-party aftermarket for swapping home-printed components?

I'll tell you what happens: We recognize that almost any consumer good is fundamentally recombinable and reproducible, the same way that music always was, and the *design* again takes primacy as the value over the good itself. One of the side effects of design taking primacy is that the selfsame fractalization of markets that results from allowing global nonfinancial exchange (i.e., each individual in a trade or barter exchange represents a unique set of interests and values, creating a dyadic market for each trade) is that mass-market goods no longer have such great value.

Another embodiment of this was that when laser cutters first became cheap enough for hobbyists and small companies to buy them, a sudden market for engraved laptop cases sprang up. Why? Because customized is always preferable to generic. With 3D printing and abundance economies for design, bespoke is now optional for everyone, meaning that creative expression is an attribute anyone can apply to any physical good. Again, this means the value is in the design, gaining value through distribution and recognition, not through scarcity.

The upshot of all this is an economy in which participation creates more value than it consumes—an abundance economy—and is the opposite of what most of us are familiar with in traditional capitalism—the scarcity economy. If I make cars, I can charge a great deal for each car, because once you buy the car nobody else can. That's the old model. But if I make the design for a laptop engraving and you use it on your laptop, anybody else can still use that design. In fact, if you use that design, it's more likely someone else will see it, like it, and use it too. The more valuable it is, the more available it is and the greater the net benefit.

That abundance economy explains the rise in everything from YouTube videos to tweets to Reddit posts. It's why Kahn Academy (a nonprofit educational website) is one of the fastest growing sources of education, why TED videos about astrophysics get passed around among millions, how Thingiverse gets so many design submissions or Etsy has new products posted hourly, or how the *Huffington Post* has so damn many authors clamoring to write for it. The abundance economy is why Justin Bieber is one of the world's biggest musicians and why Lady Gaga has so many hit singles.

It's also why PatientsLikeMe.com, a site where users share their symptoms and treatments, is a better source for R&D than anything big pharma could come up with on its own. It's why people are sending 23andMe.com, a genome-sequencing site, tubes of spit for $100 so they can share their personal physiological data with everyone else.

All of these are instances of people submitting ideas and information freely, to anyone who cares to see them, because they recognize that the more they're distributed, the more they're valuable. StackOverflow, that website where technologists compete to provide the best answer to technical questions, is huge because developers know that having a reputation for giving good answers on the site does more than make them look good—it can cement their careers, garner them respect, improve their networks, and build their programming ability. That's not bad for "free."

Even more importantly, all these models are taking off because they represent the most positive aspects of human commerce. Recognition from your peers; the potential for massive, unexpected return on an investment; feelings of belonging and contribution from a global community; and a multitude of avenues for financial and nonfinancial profit alike are all damn strong motivators.

To put it another way, I can code up a toolkit and patent it, put it on a website, and charge people $20 per download for it, and make a small amount of cash until someone writes the equivalent functionality as a derivative product and offers it for sale for less. Or I can open-source license it, distribute it freely, let my community pick it up, enjoy a reputation for writing useful code, potentially get new job offers, and have it licensed for big bucks by an industry or organization I'd never have heard of otherwise.

True, if you put it up for sale there's still the potential for recognition; the toolkit will still exist, after all. But by making it *free*, the only disincentive to trying it is if it doesn't suit someone's need or interest. This means that the potential audience of people who will take the time to check it out is significantly larger. The important difference lies in the possible return—cash versus reputation. If you have to roll the dice, why not roll for the big return? As reputation economies become larger and more diversified, that big return isn't in creating scarcity—it's in leveraging the reputation economy.

CHAPTER 8
CODE IS CULTURE

EMERGING PLATFORMS ARE RESHAPING THE
CULTURE OF COMMERCE

So what are all these new technologies and emerging models doing to real businesses? How are existing companies supposed to adapt, survive, or even thrive when everything is becoming free and infinitely reproducible?

Part of the answer lies in the fact that reputation-based economies don't function purely from the loving kindness of their participants. People can now use technology to enact a social cost on those who violate their reputation by publicizing their actions—just like giving an eBay seller a bad rating makes it harder for them to sell things on eBay. The difference is that now you can enact that sort of cost in whatever context anyone participates in, just by jumping in and becoming invested yourself. By putting your reputation on the line, you can now participate in groups you'd never have had access to before. At the same time, people are also able to step outside existing, broken systems of exchange entirely by using reputation as that same enforcing element. We're seeing new technologies emerge that facilitate all this, which may change things more than we think. By matching a stick with the carrot of reputation exchange we're seeing actionable platforms suddenly arise; not only can I sweeten the deal by allowing you to get more for your investment, I can make sure you'll take steps not to screw me in the process. That's critical when you're dealing with strangers, no matter **how** good their reputation is.

So what does this enable? Well for a start, we're starting to see barter and trade emerging as increasingly popular means of exchange. Platforms like Sharesomesugar.blogspot.com, which lets me loan my lawnmower to a distant neighbor, or borrow a pair of hedge trimmers, means that I can again rely on reputation to obtain needed goods. Knowing that if my neighbor ruins my lawnmower I can go on Sharesomesugar and make sure nobody lends to him again makes the prospect seem more viable. Bondsy.com lets you take photos of your stuff with a mobile app and then send them out to social networking friends, who can then make an offer for an exchange. While you could offer money, the site's really built to enable you to offer something nonfinancial, like helping them paint their garage in exchange for a leather chair, and again, you can rank their actions online. Or 99dresses.com, which lets users upload pictures of unwanted clothes for other users to buy with virtual currency or for trade between them. Or Kwiddy.com, which is a straight-up swap platform for musician's gear—list an item you want to trade and what you want to trade it for, and your behavior online or via their reputation system will vouch for you.

Airbnb is a more popular example. In June 2012, Airbnb hit 10 million guest nights booked worldwide since it was founded in August 2008, all based on the idea that people will let strangers stay in their homes if they have a trusted enough reputation on their platform. But it's the growth rate that's most impressive; a year prior, Airbnb hadn't yet reached 2 million nights booked. Even more significantly, the US market makes up less than half of Airbnb's total nights booked (historically), meaning that people are getting and giving lodging to people in other countries they could never have conceivably met, and they are doing it on an unprecedented scale. So far, Airbnb is active in more than 19,000 cities and 192 countries.[1] If you're looking for evidence that reputation and trust are becoming more commonplace and accepted with online platforms, it's hard to argue with numbers like that.

TWOANGAU TO KICKSTARTER TO CROWDFUNDER, OH MY!

Where did this new market come from? These methods of exchange didn't come from the ether. It turns out there's plenty of historic precedent, now adapted to online systems of scope and scale. Most of them are based on methods of exchange that have since evolved to suit the tools available. One good example comes from a few decades back in China. With increasing urban density came the emergence of Twoangau—flash-mob buying. Effectively, a large group of people (from the same apartment block, company, or club) would appear at a retail outlet and demand wholesale prices in exchange for buying in large quantities. A hundred people would appear and say, "We're each going to buy at least five gallons of paint, and pay cash, but you have to give it all to us for this many yuan per gallon." More often than not the retailer would play along, because it made good business sense to move that much stock all at once.

Fast forward to the Internet, and you get Groupon, which does basically the same thing, except at much larger scale and between much more disparate groups of people. Groupon has dozens of competitors (LivingSocial, BloomSpot, Travelzoo, Scoutmob, Saveology, Plum District, Jasmere, et cetera) offering essentially the same thing: A company can now sell "coupons" to a huge number of clients in order to make up the discounted cost through quantity. They also enjoy the profit from purchased coupons that aren't redeemed.

That same scaled model of Twoangau then gave rise to Kickstarter.com. A major success story, Kickstarter was one of the first crowd-funding sites. The way it works is, if you have a project or product you want to produce, you make a video or write a summary about it and list how much money you need to receive in donations in order to give it a go. You also list various levels of kickbacks for people who donate. So, for example, if I wanted to make a movie I could offer a free copy on DVD if you donate $10, a signed poster if you donate $20, a prescreening if you donate $100, and a cameo if you donate $1,000. Finally, you set a deadline for the funding to be complete. Then you post your Kickstarter campaign and take to your various social networks to try to get people to donate and spread the word. If you hit your goal before the time runs out, everyone has the amount they committed to donate deducted from their bank accounts or credit cards and sent to the founder, sans a small fee for Kickstarter. If you don't hit that goal, nobody loses anything.

It's a simple system, but so far it's blown all expectations out of the water—repeatedly. As just a couple of examples, video game designer Tim Schafer needed $400,000 to make a new game but wound up with $3.36 million. Musician Amanda Palmer set a goal of $100,000 for a new album and ended up with more than $1 million.[2] Time and again, critics are shocked to discover that people will gladly give away money in exchange for supporting something they really believe in. It runs counter to traditional market capitalism, in which there needs to be a clear financial return on the investment, but it fits neatly into the ideals of reputation economics. Namely, these donations are netting people important externalities such as being part of a group, identifying themselves with what they care about, helping create something they believe in, and the experience of seeing something they participated in become a real product.

Talk to anyone who's invested in Kickstarter and you'll hear something very different than if you ask them about their recent mutual fund investment. The essential motivation behind joining in on a Kickstarter campaign is more often emotional than acquisitional—it's about seeing something personally important come into the world. Reducing that transaction to dollars and cents misses the point; there's a lot of value on the table for both parties involved in the transaction—value that motivates a lot of pledges.

And I do mean a *lot*. 2012 saw 2,241,475 people pledge $319,786,629 and fund 18,109 projects. That's some incredible growth for a three-year-old company and indicates some amazing increase in interest; the amount raised in 2012 was 221 times greater than that raised in 2011, while the number of backers grew 238 percent.[3] Not surprisingly, Kickstarter is starting to have its own share of clones and similarly modeled competitors, such as Indiegogo, Peoplefund.it, RocketHub, Gambitious, Medstartr, Spot.us, GigFunder, and more.

Now, we're seeing the rise of groups like Crowdfunder.com, which does for small businesses what Kickstarter did for projects. Whereas Kickstarter allows you to invest in a project in exchange for small gifts and an opportunity to buy the resulting product, Crowdfunder is designed to take advantage of investment regulations that allow individuals of any financial background to invest in companies.

In other words, it will soon be possible to have a founder say, "I want to create a company that makes products like X. If enough people invest in my company to reach Y dollars, I'll found the company and give all the investors stock." The result is the same as with Kickstarter, Groupon, and Twoangau—everyone between the producer and the buyer is removed from the transaction. These methods of exchange mean that all the middlemen who used to exist in a transaction are suddenly subtracted, with greater value being freed up for both buyer and seller. True, in the case of crowd-funding a business, you're investing, not donating—it's not strictly for the externalities that you'd put your money into a company, especially when you know you get stock in return. But I'd argue that in the case of crowd-funding a business, those externalities would mean more than if you just bought stock in a publicly traded company on the open market, and that these platforms allow you to factor these externalities into the exchange in a way that the strictly financial platforms, such as the stock market, don't.

Overall it's a seismic shift in what "commerce" means. It perfectly matches producers and purchasers with almost zero overhead, meaning that all the trappings that made currencies necessary (guaranteed backing, representation for exchange, traceability, and so forth) vanish. Why would I buy a pair of jeans from Levi's when I can buy from the custom designer in Taiwan who specializes in the sub-sub-subculture I identify with this week, and who will sew them to my exact specifications? Sure, it may cost more, but only if it provides alternative values worth the cost—such as design. Otherwise the market drives the price to meet the demand—or the Taiwanese designer is replaced.

RETAIL, SHOWROOMING, AND THE MASS MARKET

The big argument against this, of course, is for mass market goods. But even here we see these new means and methods rapidly eroding the status quo. Best Buy, for example—the only survivor of the big commercial electronics retailer wars (of which Circuit City was a casualty)—is now suffering massive stock price degradation due to a phenomena known as "showrooming." Showrooming is where customers come to your store, browse your products, handle your goods, and make a purchasing decision. And then go home and buy it on Amazon (or whatever site offers it for the best price).

Think of any retail store, and try to imagine how showrooming isn't happening. After all, why *wouldn't* you buy online when you can do it immediately (with your phone), get it shipped to your house (often for free), and save a bundle in the process? It's the *same exact product* if it's a mass market good. The only reason to buy on the premises anymore is convenience. It's the same phenomena Barnes and Nobles bookstores combat by increasingly being the *only* physical bookstore customers have access to. Customers realize they're paying a small premium for the right to have the product immediately, and that store is the only place it can happen.

So now producers can either sell directly to individuals, investing in their reputation and relationship, or sell mass market where pricing pressures ensure that nobody will pay more than the absolute minimum, reducing margins to almost nothing. It's not a pretty picture for large-scale sellers.

BITCOIN: A FUTURE FOR MONEY

If that's not twisting your brain a little try to imagine what money could evolve into given these new market forces. Again, money as we know it emerged in many ways from the difficulties of logistically matching sellers and buyers, trading over large distances, and providing a record of transactions (among other things). But that was before the Internet. If you were to redesign money now, what would it look like? What would the nearly infinite scope and scale of a global instantaneous communication network backed by enormously powerful computational resources produce?

A lot of people think the answer is Bitcoin. A cryptographically derived currency, Bitcoin is irreproducible, does not suffer from inflation, can be exchanged in pieces down to eight decimal points, and is difficult to trace. At the moment, it's very popular in the online drug trade. It's also one of the biggest means by which Greeks are exporting their money out of Greece[4] and Iranians are removing their money from Iran.[5] Which makes sense: They're not paying their taxes, the geopolitical entity that guarantees their local currency is (some say) about to collapse, and they need to be able to pull their money out elsewhere at some other time (Bitcoin can be used to buy "real-world" currencies via multiple markets) without it being traced. Bitcoin is perfect for them...and very soon it might be for you, too.

BITCOIN, A PRIMER

Bitcoin is all over the news these days, so let's stop for a quick moment to clear up some myths about it. Bitcoin is a crypto-currency, meaning that it has several unusual characteristics that set it apart from dollars or euros. To wit:

- Bitcoin is mathematically verifiable. Basically, each bitcoin is a solution to a math problem. To "mine" bitcoins, or make more of them, you have to run a computer program that will search for a specific type of mathematical formula with a unique result. It's like finding a very, very large prime number—when you *do* find it, anyone can easily verify that the "answer" to the problem is indeed a prime number, but it takes a lot of computer power to find it in the first place.

  Ditto with bitcoins. Subsequently, a lot of people are spending a lot of computing cycles "mining" them. Firstly, because their value is currently high, and secondly in the hopes that they continue to increase in value. Recently Bitcoin increased almost 70 percent in two days, a leap attributed to the Cyprus banking crisis that drove many Europeans to invest in Bitcoin. As of this writing, Bitcoin has increased in value faster than any other currency, anywhere, ever.

  As a countervailing force to this increase in interest, however, bitcoins are designed to get harder to find the more of them there are. This means that as the market grows, the number of bitcoins that are added to the economy should slow. This is predicated on modern computing power, however. We're already seeing computer viruses designed to hijack your computer to use for mining bitcoins.

- It has a public transaction record. When I transfer money to you through my bank, the bank acts as a central authority—it flips a bit in my account that deducts the amount there, and flips a bit in your account to add it to yours. This means that we both have to wait for the bank to get around to flipping that bit, but also that we can hold the other accountable to what the central authority says is true about the bits being flipped. Bitcoin doesn't have to worry about tabulating every exchange, because anyone who owns a bitcoin can make the exchange themselves simply by publishing to the world that they've made it.

- Bitcoin has no central authority. Every bitcoin has a public record of every single transaction that's ever been done with it, available to anyone anywhere on the Internet. If I want to pass a bitcoin to you, I just enter in your account information on the record of the bitcoin itself and publish that to the Internet. I don't even need your approval; it simply becomes a matter of public record. That means that transactions are instantaneous, publicly verifiable, and extraordinarily difficult to undo, since it means I'd have to convince everyone who'd ever gotten a record of the transaction (possibly the entire Internet) to redact it.

- Bitcoin is pseudo-anonymous (versus being fully anonymous). Because of this public record, it's possible to see that the Bitcoin account for "DragonRider15" received such-and-such funds and this-and-that transaction all the way back into perpetuity. While I may not know who DragonRider15 is, and I have no way of verifying that it's an account belonging to any particular person, it *does* provide several data points that can help me narrow things down. For example, DragonRider15 may have transacted with Merchant X, who shipped the cigarettes bought in bitcoins to a certain physical address. If I can get that address from Merchant X, I can find out who lives at the address and then figure out who DragonRider15 is.

The upshot of all this is that if I wanted to "launder" money through Bitcoin transactions I could do it, programmatically (and therefor automatically), by moving large transactions into progressively smaller ones and then running those into and out of accounts in other currencies. At that point it becomes an arms race of traceability through all the varied accounts, because each point at which a Bitcoin transaction occurs is logged, even if only through a shell account, and is therefore traceable. In other words, it's not easy and it's time consuming and expensive to both launder and trace. But it's not impossible. So, pseudo-anonymous.

- Bitcoins are bounded. They have a "hard" limit of 21 million bitcoins, which should be reached by the year 2140. However, clients can divide each bitcoin down to eight decimal places (a total of 2.1×1015 or 2.1 quadrillion units derived from the 21 million total Bitcoins). This means that once we hit 21 million bitcoins, they can be further subdivided to account for inflation of the pool.

- The U.S. Treasury's Financial Crimes Enforcement Network issued a statement in March 2013 about virtual currencies making it clearer that individual Bitcoin users—and Bitcoin miners—would not be regulated.[6] Exchanges, on the other hand, look like they will need to get a money transmitter license. What's more, FinCEN, the US Dept. of Treasury's Financial Crimes

Enforcement Network, specifically says that miners fall under their regulations. This means that more folks will be mining bitcoins offshore, and that while individuals can continue to use Bitcoin without hesitation, transferring your bitcoins to another currency may have to happen outside the United States and then be transferred back—which will certainly set back Bitcoin, the United States, or both.

Here's the rub: All the seemingly criminal elements of Bitcoin also make it perfect for calculated exchanges online. Why use dollars, or yen, or euros, or any other fiat currency when the price of a good in Bitcoin is not subject to government inflation and is derived directly from market demand? For that matter, why would you buy anything in dollars or yen or euros when it demands you pay transfer fees, wait days for the transaction to appear on record so you can account for it, work with clunky and outdated bureaucratic regulations, and maintain fragile and expensive accounts with institutions you don't trust just to allow yourself to make the purchase? Bitcoin, while a new, risky, and untested method of value transfer, seems to circumvent those problems.

An interesting thought experiment here is to consider what it would take to make Bitcoin widely accepted for mainstream use. Most of the experts I've consulted with have all agreed that the main thing stopping that from happening is easy exchange into and out of local currencies—points of exchange—and vendors accepting it.

Right now our countries' currencies are so prevalent, and financial exchange so ubiquitous, that most of us don't do a lot of currency exchange in day-to-day life. But that could change pretty easily. Really, this exchange could be made fundamentally invisible to us, with funds being transferred into bitcoin before a transaction took place, and back out again as soon as it was completed. Because transactions can happen nearly instantaneously, this is perfectly suited to being a background activity facilitated by an intelligent device such as your phone. (Note that making your phone your wallet is the holy grail of every cell phone manufacturer on the planet.) The upside? All the same advantages of Bitcoin.

At that point, all it takes is vendors who will accept Bitcoin. If you thought a good place to start might be vendors who have a website (which is a fair number of them), then rest assured the transformation is already well underway. In April 2013, the Web Hypertext Application Technology Working Group ratified the "bitcoin:" label for the HTML5 specification.

In case that doesn't make your heart race, let me explain why it should. The HTML specification is the standard for the code that web pages (all of them) run on. HTML5 is the latest iteration, and the "bitcoin:" label would allow anyone to add a link on their web page. You know how some links on some sites automatically pop up your e-mail client with a new e-mail where the "To:" field is already populated with an e-mail address? It's often a link that looks like an e-mail address itself, and it makes it super easy for you to send an e-mail—just click, and then you can write whatever you want to whomever is supposed to receive it using a program you're comfortable with.

The "bitcoin:" label does exactly that for Bitcoin. Essentially, if you want to buy something online, all you have to do is click the link, which would open up whatever Bitcoin wallet software you're using, and bang!—you can buy it in Bitcoin.

That's a huge shift toward making Bitcoin dead easy to use for purchasing online, and if its use becomes widely popularized, it's not a big leap from there to platforms like Square, PayPal, Stripe, and other transaction platforms (like the aforementioned cell phone) becoming more widely integrated as points of sale (POS) in the real world. When that happens, the reasons *not* to use Bitcoin start becoming negligible. The "barrier to entry," as they say in business, is rapidly getting smaller and smaller.

There's another element to existing systems of exchange that's indicative of how our technology is starting a sea change for commerce. If you lived in the United States, why would you pay a premium for an electric razor on Amazon when you could order it from a UK computer address (via a VPN, for example) to be shipped to your US postal address and get it for the cheaper UK price? You'd only do that because an artificial limitation (a decision by Amazon that those in the United States should pay more for that particular razor than those in the United Kingdom) was enforced in some way you couldn't easily get around. That type of limitation is increasingly fragile and difficult to enforce as we all realize there are simple technical ways to get around them.

THE RISING INTEREST IN CIRCUMVENTION TECHNOLOGIES

The recent Olympic games in London illustrate this nicely. NBC promised "real-time" viewing of the Olympic games to a huge audience across the United States. But by "real time" they meant "real time plus four to six hours so we can show it during prime time and recoup maximum marketing dollars." Everyone who wanted to watch the games who also spent time online quickly discovered they'd been lied to as the traffic on Twitter and Facebook started streaming by, celebrating victories, bemoaning defeats, and basically spoiling every event hours before it was visible to the US audience.[7]

So a huge percentage of the United States suddenly became interested in circumventing NBC's viewing restrictions. The use of VPNs (virtual private networks) shot through the roof as viewers discovered they could "plug in" to the Internet from Sweden, France, or any of hundreds of other locations that had access to true live-streaming footage of the games.

In this way, a massive percentage of the United States suddenly discovered how to route around the "damage" of geocorporate content restrictions, the same way that millions suddenly discovered how to use BitTorrent or Limewire to download music once the RIAA destroyed Napster, the premier free music sharing platform of its day. Again and again, we see new platforms emerging—and emerging faster and faster—to address people's needs and wants where the existing solutions don't provide. It's simple evolution in response to demand, except that the incumbent institutions that stand to profit are sitting around with their thumbs in their ears while it happens.

What's this have to do with Bitcoin? Those same technologies and platforms that are increasingly widely used to circumvent existing restrictions like geographic pricing schemes mean that alternative platforms now have the opportunity to provide better services for better prices—even when those services or prices are obtained against the interests of the corporations who seek to restrict them. It seems likely that those platforms will need a currency that cannot be restricted by the same geopolitical entities that wanted to enforce "typical" commercial exchange in the first place. Right now that market is primarily made up of drug trades and virtual goods purchases, but that won't be the case for long. And when it changes, Bitcoin (or something like it) is set to become the true coin of the realm.

Essentially, Bitcoin takes the fact that online reputation is now a legitimate, scalable means of evaluating an exchange and wraps it in a mechanism that meshes nicely with our ideas about the mechanics of commerce. Anonymity isn't a problem because we have cryptographic evidence of authenticity, meaning that we don't need to rely on a nation-state to prove that we're paying the same person who promised to deliver a good. That cryptographic reliance is new but also negligible to anyone who's spent any time online. Instead, the trick is that we can "pay" a certain amount of a thing (bitcoins) to another person and trace the transaction, which is all very familiar, and then transfer that thing to any other currency we choose, like dollars, if and when we want to. Now bitcoins, which are essentially very complex math problems wrapped in a bundle of otherwise obtuse code and distributed record systems, are the same as any other currency. That means that we can use them just like we've always used dollars, *with* any system that uses dollars. That's about as smooth an on-ramp to replacing modern currency with a cryptocurrency as you could want, and it's sweetened with plenty of benefits to make it worth doing.

It's the same track that we're seeing taken by other technologies, from using VPNs to watch shows that are banned in your region, to downloading music, to the increasing primacy of design. The utility of reputation is taking otherwise obtuse, difficult-to-understand technologies and transforming them into something intuitive and immediately useful. As that happens, we're seeing a shift back to historic methods of exchange meshed tightly with new technical capabilities, creating something truly disruptive to the existing financial model.

CHAPTER 9
EMERGING MODELS...
AND MARKETS

TECHNOLOGY REVOLUTION EVOLUTION

The good news is that it turns out this confluence of emerging technology, dissolving business models, and aggressively anti-authoritarian self-aggregators is actually turning up some pretty great stuff. Reputation economies are prompting enormous shifts in how commerce is viewed. At the same time, strong motivators to abandon existing systems are reaching critical mass while platforms to develop and demonstrate alternatives are proliferating.

The result is a variety of enormously accelerated steps toward utilizing reputation economics in ways that more strongly benefit users. Not all of these are practical—in fact, I'd say most of them are soon-to-die middle steps on the way to a more integrated, broadly available set of options for commerce available to everybody. But any one of them could gain substantial ground or set the stage for an emerging new standard of exchange.

We're all actively participating in this revolution already, without being fully aware of it, and we somehow think it's the most natural evolution in the world as it happens around us. That's how technological revolution happens—can you imagine life without television, or radio, or the printed page? Not seeing these changes because they're so organic makes a lot of sense, but it can also be damaging when we're caught unawares. The question now is if (and how) these changes can benefit you.

CREATIVE COMMONS AND FREE AND OPEN SOURCE SOFTWARE

We've already talked about gift economies historically, and it turns out that being able to connect globally with anyone who shares an interest has only grown their viability. Free or Open Source Software (F/OSS) like Linux, Apache, Mozilla, Gimp, Sun's Java, OpenOffice, and more are examples of programs licensed specifically to emphasize free (as in free speech—with little or no restriction) versus free (as in free beer—for zero price). A survey of 740 software development company representatives done in 2012 indicated that by 2017, 50 percent of all software purchases will be F/OSS.[1] At the moment there are more than 600,000 F/OSS projects in the wild. Every day, GitHub (a cloud service for hosting projects in development) sees roughly 25,000 *new* repositories created.[2] So clearly, open source is proving a powerful alternative to centralized development companies such as Microsoft or Oracle.

This makes a lot of sense. Software is cheap to develop, there are almost limitless niche markets to develop for, and getting a reputation for developing good software can net you some pretty lucrative work. It also makes a lot of sense to *use*; a recent study examined 278 million web server log records to see who was using F/OSS in which companies. What they found was that there were "statistically significant differences on gross margins and (positive) profits between users and non-users of F/OSS."[3] So it seems that using F/OSS can lead to more profitable businesses as well.

The same model is expanding outside of just software. Works licensed under the Creative Commons (CC) are also growing increasingly popular. From journalist organizations like Al Jazeera or the Pulitzer Prize–winning ProPublica and renowned authors like Dan Gillmor to the Open University and TED talks; from the open source hardware platform Arduino to the innumerable number of artists who freely share their creations through platforms like Jamendo; from nongovernmental organizations like Human Rights Watch to leading car manufacturers like Fiat, the Creative Commons schema has had impressive growth, which can be summarized at last count as more than 400 million total CC-licensed works as of 2010 (that we know of—because they don't have to be registered with anyone, the actual number is likely much, much higher).

Functionally, the CC license lets you place a variety of restrictions on your work—such as only allowing distribution with attribution, so you'll always be credited for your work while allowing others to give away copies for free. You can also require that anyone be allowed to remix, rework, redistribute, or otherwise alter the work in any way they want *as long as they don't use it commercially*. If they want to make money on it, they have to license it from you. The main advantage of this model—similar to F/OSS—is that it encourages distribution, which means you can accrue reputation.

I used this model for my first book, a science fiction novel called *R'ood*. As a new author I had roughly a snowball's chance in hell of scoring a book deal with a major publisher, so instead I released it under a Creative Commons Attribution-Noncommercial-Share Alike 3.0 License[4] with the idea that it would at least give me a chance at gaining some readership. I slapped the license on my manuscript, posted it to my website, and exactly nothing happened. Well, not nothing—my mom downloaded a copy.

Then I discovered that the iPhone had been hacked (this was before the iPhone app store) and that there was an illegal e-book reader—the first for the iPhone!—available to install. My commute at the time took me out of cell coverage via the subway for a good 30 to 40 minutes a day, and losing the weight of dead-tree media for that trip sounded pretty good, so I leaped at the chance to install prohibited software on my phone despite the risk of turning it into a paperweight. The software worked, and I soon opened the e-book reader to discover that it came with one book only—*Tarzan*.

Now, *Tarzan* is a great book, but it occurred to me that the kind of guy who was willing to hack their expensive smartphone and install potentially fatal software on it wasn't the prime demographic for *Tarzan*. But *I* was that guy, and I'd written a book I thought was pretty cool. So I contacted the person who'd bundled the e-book reader and asked if he'd include my novel. It was, after all, CC-licensed, so all he had to do was download a copy from my website. He agreed, and I sat back happy in the knowledge that maybe a few people would end up reading my book after all.

Then I started getting e-mail from people who'd read the book and wanted to know if I was doing a sequel. And then straight-up fan mail. And then e-mails from people who wanted to know where they could donate money to me as a way of saying thanks for writing it. And then people who wanted to translate it into other languages. Based on the numbers we got, more than *20,000* people downloaded my novel the very first month it was made available.

Because it is CC-licensed, people started posting it elsewhere on the Internet, and suddenly I was being contacted by folks who'd found it on platforms I'd never heard of, in countries I'd never heard of. Because I didn't have centralized control I can't say how many people actually read the book, but based on e-mail feedback, it was *significantly* more than 20,000/month those next few months!

That initial bump eventually slowed down, but—and this is the interesting part—it never fully went away. I *still* get people contacting me about *Roo'd* almost half a decade later! And because I made it available for purchase via Amazon's print-on-demand service, I still make money from its sales. Not much (I could probably cover lunch once a month on the proceeds, if I eat cheap), but something. Five years after giving away my sci-fi novel for free, without doing any marketing whatsoever.

That's not addressing all the ancillary benefits of reputation, either. At a conference I once had a woman approach me to mention she'd read the novel and really liked it before asking me to join her and her companion, a head of state, for dinner. At another event I was supposed to convince a group of 15-year-olds who were deeply, disgustedly unimpressed with the idea of listening to an adult lecture on cybersecurity. When it came out I'd written cyberpunk—and a novel that a couple of them had read—I suddenly became "okay."

There are a number of other nonfinancial advantages, and the book continues to garner all of them because it's free to give away to anyone who might conceivably be interested. In fact, it was partly on the basis of the popularity of that novel that I got a decent advance for my second book. I hadn't planned this success—really, I was prepared to consign my first novel to a shoebox under my bed—but decided to try a CC license instead because it was dead easy and free to use. The returns have been substantial...because of the reputation economy.

NEW PLATFORMS AND GIFT ECONOMIES

What's interesting about this is that the communities that use licenses like CC and F/OSS very often function as gift economies. Once a work can be infinitely reproduced for negligible cost, as is so often the case with digital products, a lot of the value comes from recognition from peers and reciprocation of effort. Because there's no explicit contract for using a work that's "free," there has to be a cultural mechanism for ensuring a return on investment. Gift economies—in terms of people building on your work, lauding it publicly, and offering aid in exchange—is a perfect means for achieving this.

StackOverflow is again a perfect example. Beyond being a way for programmers to show off their chops to each other, it's become a means through which potential employers are able to reliably evaluate programmers' capabilities. Because an employer is unlikely to know the intricacies of my particular field of interest or participation, how my work is judged by a community of my peers is an extraordinarily good means of evaluating my response to technical questions as well as a test of my overall technical competence in that field. It's also an indicator of how well respected I am in that same field—an element which is equally as important in making a hire.

But the gift economy element also plays a major component. Contributing to StackOverflow raises your esteem in your peers' eyes, meaning that when *you* have a question, your chance of getting it answered—and answered quickly and well—is greatly increased. It's another example of an abundance economy: The more you contribute, the more value there is available to you.

This sort of gift economy isn't limited to the online world. It's increasingly being recognized as a viable means of obtaining and exchanging value in the real world. One neatly defined example is the Burning Man festival that takes place in a temporary city in the remote Nevada desert for eight days leading up to Labor Day. Marina Gorbis at the Institute for the Future says, "There are lots of gift economies going on where people don't measure things in commodity terms, but rather as methods of incentivizing to give and share. Behavioral economics and neuroscience have both shown that giving things away increases satisfaction, and Burning Man is a great big engine for giving. The more you give the more respected you are and the more satisfaction you get, whether that be water, a grilled cheese sandwich, or a great performance."[5]

The same dynamic that exists in the microcosm of Burning Man is a very real potential for the rest of the world. "There are pockets of this that have always existed, but people are becoming more conscious of it," says Gorbis. "In the age of austerity which a lot of cities are living in we haven't figured out a good mechanism for distribution yet. We have totally abundant resources for everything—in many places the reason people experience poverty is a distribution issue. We have extra food, housing, and people are sitting on those resources instead of socializing them. If we could figure out a mechanism for sharing it might solve a lot of these issues."

Gorbis isn't just hand-waving about this. The Institute for the Future recently opened their office for co-working, meaning that strangers were free to come and use underutilized desk space, Wi-Fi, air-conditioning, and more. "By socializing an underutilized resource you bring tremendous value to not only the people who use it, but also to the people who give it—we've benefitted tremendously through the exposure to the people that have used our space by accessing their expertise, enthusiasm, and connections."

This exact same mechanism is happening increasingly frequently across the country, not only with shared workspaces, but through hackathons, festivals, community workshops, and more. One element of the shared resource gift economy that has been often overlooked is that in a lot of places where these things have not been monetized people *have* to use nonfinancial systems; if there is only one water well and nobody has any money, keeping a system of dollars in debt to the well doesn't make any sense. The same goes for care of the elderly, or for what have become—in many parts of the First World—highly professionalized chores, like childcare or education.

In other words, it's only because the First World *has* monetized most things that we feel we *need* to be able to calculate everything in dollars or euros. For much of the rest of the world, that's not only untrue, it's an offensive reduction of the actual value of the service. That realization, or shift in values, is happening slowly and intuitively across the First World as the software we socialize with makes it easier to participate with others in reputation exchanges. Without even noticing it, we're beginning to see reputation exchanges as normal.

PAYING WITH TIME

Take time banking as an example. Time-based currency systems were first instituted in London in 1832 by Robert Owen, a Welsh socialist and labor reformer. Since then time banking communities can be found in more than 37 nations on six continents.

The idea behind time banking is simple. You put in one hour's labor, and you get one "time dollar" (or whatever the system calls its units of measurement). You can then later take those dollars and spend them on time from other people. So, for example, you could earn an hour helping the community center set up their computer system, and then later spend that hour to use their gym. Or to have the local baker make you a cake. Or get a massage, or a bushel of oranges, or whatever else the system supports. In this case, the fundamental unit is time, which is then tallied up as time dollars.

Because everyone's time is equally valued regardless of skill—an hour of brain surgery is worth the same amount as an hour of weeding—time dollars encourage reciprocation within the community that uses it. Given that the value of a time dollar is fixed at one hour, it is resistant to inflation and doesn't earn interest. That means there's no reason to hoard it, which lends it attributes of a gift economy (in which the only value is in the giving, rather than the static potential, of the currency). Finally, because there is always time with which to create more time dollars, it is always in sufficient supply, which allows for scalable trade and cooperation among participants.

In most instances time banking is used to provide incentives for work such as mentoring children, caring for the elderly, or just being neighborly; work usually done by volunteers and which a pure market system inherently devalues. As a result, communities often use time banking as a tool to forge stronger intra-community connections.

All is not wine and roses with time banking, however. One of the problems is it heavily relies on trust. You can easily be a slacker in donating time and cash it out from someone acting in earnest. It also values everyone's time the same, which tends to limit it to certain sorts of participants. After all, if I were the aforementioned brain surgeon, I'd still rather do brain surgery for $200/ hour and then use ordinary dollars rather than trade my labor for an hour of weeding. Perhaps that's why most time banks are so ferociously localized—by physically participating in a community you increase the potential costs for defrauding the system. I.e., if it's easy for your neighbors to notice you're screwing the time bank, they're going to make you pay for it *somehow*.

Interestingly, time banking seems to be taking off in places like Spain and Greece, where the countries' economies are doing poorly and unemployment is high.[6] The number of time banks in Spain has nearly doubled over the past two years to 291, according to a survey by Julio Gisbert, a banker who runs a site that tracks mutual-aid initiatives.[7]

Southern Europe's other troubled economies are showing similar efforts. In one town hundreds of people use a currency called the TEM (an acronym for "Local Alternative Unit"). Time banks are popping up in Modena and other parts of Italy, mobilized to help people affected by earthquakes. Where it is used, you get strikingly similar responses. "Having a network of support like this is really important at a time when you're vulnerable," says Alessandra Melis, 30, a housekeeper in Spain. Carlos Bravo, a 35-year-old information technician also in Spain, says, "They're people you can count on, and in this time of economic crisis, for people who lack the resources to get things on their own, they know there are people here to give a helping hand."[8]

It's hard to get your head around, but from being a fringe network system to becoming an important economy used in countries where the national financial system is failing the population, time banking suddenly became normal for a big swath of people in a variety of countries.

Of course, there's a potential downside to banking with currencies that are basically commodified favors only exchangeable within predesignated trust relationship networks. Many economists hasten to point out that the growth of such informal systems of economic exchange is pushing more and more otherwise taxable income underground, into darknets and shadow economies where governments can neither measure nor monitor. Even now, time banks in the United States must avoid setting any monetary worth on their time dollars, lest it become taxable income to the IRS.

VIRTUAL CURRENCIES: NOT NEW AFTER ALL

We've already talked about Bitcoin, one of the big contenders for the alternative currency throne. But it's important to note that Bitcoin has significant precedent; e-gold, WebMoney, and many others. The ven—a currency that first appeared as an application on Facebook on July 4, 2007, and is available in financial markets via a partnership with Thomson Reuters Indices—trades against other major currencies at floating exchange rates and is valuated on the financial markets from a basket of currencies, commodities, and carbon futures. For that matter, linden dollars and *World of Warcraft* coins (both currencies used in online games) can be exchanged in (sometimes illegal) online marketplaces for goods and services.

The point is that virtual currencies are nothing new. Extralegal, semilegal, legitimized through partnership with Thomson Reuters, or useful simply by virtue of the fact that everyone in your neighborhood respects them, the idea of "dollars" or any other unit of value being exchangeable isn't exactly rocking the boat. Instead, it's replicating (in most cases) existing systems of centralized currency exchange, and (in some cases, as with Bitcoin) offering a very similar model to existing financial systems with some small (but sometimes significant, such as through being decentralized) changes.

A META-CURRENCY FRAMEWORK

That too, is changing. Take Ripple, for example. While not widely implemented, Ripple was designed as a "system of free banking that separates the payment routing function from the credit aggregation function."[9] Based on the structure of the Internet itself, it treats every participant as a "node" that can pass tokens of value (like bitcoins, dollars, vens, or whatever) to one another. Basically, it allows debts and credits to be shuffled around, so you only owe or pay debts to persons you already trust—so if I want to buy something from a stranger, it chains together trusted parties until I can owe someone I know, who then owes someone they know, who then owes the stranger I bought from (who they know).

To make this concrete, let's say Ted, Kevin, Nancy, and I went to a restaurant together. Ted is Kevin's friend, Kevin is Nancy's friend, and Nancy is my friend. At the end of the night, Ted pays the bill with his credit card. I don't know Ted and don't want to owe him anything. Neither does Nancy. Kevin is fine owing Ted, since they already have a trust relationship. So I pay (or owe) Nancy, who pays (or owes) Kevin, who pays (or owes) Ted. Each person only exchanges according to their existing trust relationships.

Where this gets interesting is in the case of existing debt. Let's say that in the above example Kevin already owed Nancy $20, and the dinner bill was $100 (split four ways, that means each person owed $25). When I paid (or owed) Nancy $25, she then owed Kevin $50 (for both herself and I). Except that the prior debt of $20 can then be applied, meaning she now only owes Kevin $30—of which I just paid (or owe) her $25. So her total loss or debt is down to $5.

The reason that's of interest is it means that the more you trade with others, the more reason you have to keep trading with them—to manage your respective debts with amounts owed you. In other words, it suddenly starts looking a lot like a quantified gift economy made available via a convenient online platform.

It's also relevant particularly when you start including different kinds of value and exchange. If I have trades in bitcoins, dollars, euros, and vens, I can start paying debts or incurring them in whatever way will net me the best return from the person I'm exchanging with. And the broader my network, the more options for exchange I have.

In other words, Ripple would allow me to (theoretically) become a dynamic market trader with as large a network as I can establish via trust. That's an important consideration given that online reputation networks allow the outer bounds of that network to expand beyond the people I can actually "know" in the old-fashioned face-to-face sense. And perhaps more importantly, it's a system that some very savvy investors have decided to put some very serious cash behind.

Ripple's sponsor company, OpenCoin, recently received a significant amount of investment from some well-known angel funders, including Andreessen Horowitz. (Horowitz has invested in Facebook, Groupon, Twitter, Zynga, Airbnb, Foursquare, and others—ventures that have done pretty well for themselves.) While their implementation of Ripple is significantly more productized than the original design, it's still an amazing endorsement of the system. Chief among the reasons for the investment was that Ripple doesn't need currency exchanges: it is its own distributed currency exchange, allowing anyone to accept hard cash for their ripples.

These people aren't investing in OpenCoin because they think it's cute—most angel investors anticipate a *minimum* of ten times their investment in return. That's some serious confidence that the framework (or something very similar to it) is going to get major traction. It's a big jump from the days when my hacker friends and I would huddle around the back of a bar fervently assuring each other that someday cryptocurrency frameworks and darknet transaction mechanisms would become mainstream. As they say on the street (I'm told), Andreesson Horowitz's investment is a big sign that alternative currency frameworks "just got real."

A BANKING FRAMEWORK FOR NONBANKED CURRENCIES

Ripple isn't the only system operating in this space. Monetas is another currency-agnostic exchange system designed to allow digital finance entrepreneurs to start up micropayment services, financial markets, community currencies, and escrow services (among other things) without needing traditional banking or legal systems.

As Johann Gevers, Monetas' CEO, says, "You can use fiat currencies, digital gold currencies, Bitcoin, basket currencies, or the most sophisticated derivatives. Our system works with any asset type."[10]

What's most interesting about the Monetas software is that it doesn't use a database, but rather uses digitally signed receipts. In any exchange, the receipts have to be signed by all parties to be valid, making it nearly impossible for any of the parties to cheat. The software underlying Monetas uses cryptography to create unforgeable transactions and balances for each exchange.

In the Monetas system there is no centralized service keeping track of all this. Similar to Bitcoin, each receipt *is* the asset being traded, as well as being evidence of the legitimacy of the exchange. All any user needs to prove his asset balances is a copy of his last transaction receipt, which can't be created without getting all members of the exchange to cryptographically agree to its validity.

This means that an entity using the Monetas software can provide all the usual banking services—accounts, checks, transaction receipts, et cetera—without needing a centralized database. Nothing is forgeable, so it doesn't have to act as an authority certifying the legitimacy of the transactions. That's a huge advantage when you consider how geopolitical entities like nation states might want to start restricting virtual currencies. If "banks" can spring up without needing anything more than software and trust, it suddenly puts the kibosh on a whole lot of regulatory bodies and middlemen who would otherwise be collecting a paycheck—and taxes.

On the face of it this idea seems a little crazy—most of us aren't *that* opposed to paying taxes. But consider how many transactions you make in daily life where you probably are legally obligated to pay taxes or fees, but don't. The kid next door who mowed your lawn. The lady selling cookies at the festival in the park. Each of these examples are black market exchanges, and we don't think anything of them; they're just part of how our life in commerce works.

That's exactly what Monetas builds on, taking that same convenience and momentum of sociocultural expectation and extending it, just a little, onto the global Internet. Want to transfer some funds to your friend in Whatsituanialand? You *could* do it through your bank, but it'd take a really long time, cost a lot in fees, and be a huge hassle. Or you could just use Monetas and whatever platform is convenient for you and do it instantaneously—just like using a bank, but so much easier! And also, coincidentally, tax free.

Welcome, comrade, to the revolution.

COMMUNITY-DRIVEN SPENDING

Another area in which a great deal of participation is happening is in spending allocated by and from the crowd. While not necessarily democratic, the scale at which community engagement engender large data sets that can be publicly measured and used to drive smart spending is increasing radically.

For example, PinkArmy.org is a community-driven, open source cooperative aimed at changing how breast cancer drugs are developed. They take all the funding from a particular period and use it to create one treatment for one case, then turn around and make all the information learned available to the public at large. Essentially, they take everyone who participates and use their contributions to help determine where to invest their resources.

PatientsLikeMe.com does a similar thing, albeit as a second level effect, for the pharmaceutical industry. By providing clear, measurable evidence of where individuals are participating most in self-motivated treatment research—and where existing drug therapies are falling—pharmaceutical companies can see exactly where there are holes in the market or opportunities for investment.

As an example of this principle playing out directly with the consumer, Everland Clothing is a store that doesn't usually have a store. Instead, it's an online community 400,000 members strong that has already raised $1.1 million to control everything about its products. Instead of sourcing from large-scale suppliers, it designs its own clothes, sources materials directly from the manufacturers—such as cashmere from Mongolia—and makes decisions about what to produce based primarily on feedback from its community.[11] The result is articles such as a $50 designer T-shirt available for $15.

It's exactly as natural as voicing your opinion at a party about what sort of pizza to order. With a little luck, everyone gets a better result. Why wouldn't you share your opinion and information if it's going to help everyone (including yourself) at no expense? Again, it's intuitive, and as the returns get greater and greater the more people participate, it gets even more so.

PREDICTION MARKETS

Less popular (among big companies and governments) are prediction markets. Have you ever heard the adage that if you ask enough people how many jellybeans are in a given jar and averaged the responses, you'd get the exact answer? It's essentially a confidence estimate (one in which reputation plays a big role), and it's the concept behind prediction markets. Essentially, a market might give you a dollar if a certain presidential candidate is elected, so an individual who thinks she had a 70 percent chance of knowing who will be elected would be willing to pay up to 70 cents to secure their bet.

The way this plays out is like any other market; people who buy low and sell high are rewarded (and coincidentally improve the market prediction), while those who buy high and sell low are punished for degrading the market prediction. Interestingly, "evidence so far suggests that prediction markets are at least as accurate as other institutions predicting the same events with a similar pool of participants."[12]

There are lots of ways these markets can be used, or even informally simulated. "A credit default swap price is a market estimate of how likely a country is to default on bonds. It's an estimate of how much trust exists in the likelihood of a country not defaulting," says Patri Friedman, an American activist and theorist of political economy.[13] The grandson of Nobel Prize–winning economist Milton Friedman and economist Rose Friedman, and son of economist and physicist David D. Friedman, Patri has a storied background on which to base his estimates.

"Even though it's expressed in purely mathematical terms, that's a reputation, and one that can help people become aware of a crisis earlier," says Friedman. "Same goes for the prices of bank stocks and bonds, which express the market reputation of the bank's mortgage holdings, and in this case [the US housing bubble] it played a significant role in the awareness of what was happening. Essentially, a bank can tell everyone they're fine, but if the value of their stock drops in half, or if the price of insuring their bonds triples, that's a sign that the market thinks there's a problem."

Essentially, reputation can counterweigh the bad models being used to justify the behaviors of the bank. But again, that doesn't make them popular with the people making money off those models—even a casual observer of the US housing bubble can see how the people who were most invested in the bad mortgages worked the hardest to convince everyone that everything was ok. It was in their interest to obscure what many in the market were already suggesting—and which prediction markets (informal or otherwise) were already suggesting was a disaster in the making.

This is just plain measurement, and measurement of data and information that is increasingly freely available. In one case, Robin Hanson, an associate professor of economics at George Mason University and a research associate at the Future of Humanity Institute of Oxford University, wants to make a formal prediction market on how much a company's value will increase if they fire the CEO.[14] "In this case it becomes a measure of how much trust exists in the CEO," says Friedman. "The difference is between branding as making a perception of your country and branding as in measuring the actual value of your brand."

That's a scary concept for corporate leaders. Giving the public— or even general shareholders—access to hard, substantive numbers on the communities' predictive value of the CEO is a far cry from the traditional golden parachute. Nevertheless, this is exactly what companies like Amazon or Google are doing for individuals in calculating their value as advertising targets—especially as they begin to dynamically adjust prices accordingly. In a way, it's holding executives and corporate share prices accountable to the same standards and metrics they're using to evaluate their consumers. Which isn't to say they like it.

"CEOs tend to hate prediction models," says Tim Sullivan, editor at Harvard Business Review and author of *The Org: The Underlying Logic of the Office*. "They're supposed to be 'the expert,' even though their position is very often less about expertise and more about your place in the hierarchy."

Of course, companies *could* use prediction models to their advantage. Sullivan explains, "One way around it that some organizations use is that those tools enhance expertise rather than challenge it; they provide a broader range of things to make decisions on and narrows the range to investigate. So for example, you could use predictive markets to determine the top five choices for investing in soy, and then use expertise to make a final decision."[15]

Put another way, prediction markets are a way of deriving indicators of a public's perception of a company, executive, product, or anything else. It's a statistically validated estimation of reputation—what companies like Klout and Kred have been trying to infer through online behavior, except in this case explicitly gathered by motivating participants to wager on their opinions. It's not certain—it's a bet, like any other investment—but it's also a powerful tool. Ostensibly, it could be used widely for all kinds of things where public opinion is a good indicator of value, potential, or behavior.

But that's not what usually happens. In fact, prediction markets have become so reviled that just 20 days after the 2012 election, the US Commodity Futures Trading Commission (CFTC) shut down Intrade, the most recognized prediction market in the United States. A piece in *Science* journal, about the "Promise of Prediction Markets," written by a group of scientists including three Nobel Laureates (Ken Arrow, Thomas Schelling, and Vernon Smith), explains why: "Unfortunately, however, current federal and state laws limiting gambling create significant barriers to the establishment of vibrant, liquid prediction markets in the United States. We believe that regulators should lower these barriers by creating a legal safe harbor for specified types of small stakes markets, stimulating innovation in both their design and their use."[16]

In other words, the fact that there is no regulatory approval for crowd-generated predictions on the outcome of wars, market crashes, and election results means that it cannot be allowed; after all, if it isn't profitable for the existing elite, and can prove disruptive to their power structures, what else is there to do except outlaw it?

The caveat there, of course, is that outlawing it is likely to force it to improve, which might just make it impossible to stop. Like weasels imported to Hawaii to kill all the snakes, what seems like a sensible move to protect the existing power structure might have unforeseen side effects. The same way weasels started killing all the birds in Hawaii because they have no natural predators there, the downside to continually prohibiting useful mechanisms like prediction markets here might be that it forces them to improve to the point where *not* using them no longer makes sense.

FUNDED BY THE CROWD

On the other side of the fence are communities whose structure is defined by how the money is spent. Rather than participating to the point of making a group decision on allocating funds, people explicitly allocate funds and allow that to define the group. It's the idea behind the free market, and it is the defining counterpoint to prediction markets or platforms like PatientsLikeMe.com. Whereas the latter are being pushed down by the existing power elite, the former is embraced as the "invisible hand" of the market voting with its dollars. If you spend your money to request a change, it's likely to be more respected than if you only spend your money for the change you've requested.

This wouldn't be so problematic if it didn't look like the heart of innovation was boarding a one-way express train directly to crowds as a source of funding and expertise. The Jumpstart Our Business Startups (JOBS) act was signed into law on April 2012 by President Barack Obama, and was eventually modified to include a "startup exemption" designed to make it legal for entrepreneurs to use crowd-funding to raise some early-stage, equity-based financing.

An amendment made by the Senate altered the crowd-funding exception to require intermediaries in a crowd-funded offering to be registered with the SEC, and President Obama seems ready to sign once it's passed by both chambers. The SEC had a deadline to issue the regulations on January 2013, but as of this writing it's still not been finalized. If it passes, companies like Crowdfunder. com or ProFounder.com could offer to startup investing the same breadth of scale and deep access to crowds that Kickstarter.com has employed to phenomenal success.

Why does this matter? Ken Howery, one of the original cofounders of PayPal and current cofounder of Founders Fund, had a few words on the topic. "It's a huge win from a fairness point of view," said Howery. "It's very possible this changes everything."[17]

Howery would know. He's built—and invested—in some of the biggest and best technology companies out there. As we've seen from companies like Kickstarter, there's a tremendous appetite for young, entrepreneurial ventures serving niche as well as broadly based needs. Crowd-funding isn't a panacea—there are definitely serious potential downfalls, both from an investor standpoint and from a company management point of view. If you know nothing about investing, it's quite possible you could be very bad at it, and blow all your money as a result. But that problem already exists—lotteries are enormously popular despite copious mathematical proof that they're terrible, terrible investments.

Conversely, accepting investment through crowd-funding might not be a walk in the park either. As Howery notes, "Crowdsourcing could create a significant hassle for the founders by having so many investors."[18] In other words, too many cooks in the kitchen may not make for very good soup.

But overall, allowing the course of innovation—in terms of who gets funding, and how much—to be steered by popular opinion marks a radical departure from business as usual in the known world. Money follows money, goes the old adage, except that now that doesn't necessarily hold true. Now, money may follow what people want to see built. It's a radical departure from the Wall Street world of ivory tower experts (sometimes) predicting the fickle course of economics.

CROWD-JUDGING HR

It's not just in investing that this is happening, either. It's a phenomenon we're even seeing in hiring, and not just in the ad hoc means of judging people by their StackOverflow contributions. DeveloperAuction.com allows developers to submit their information and then holds bimonthly auctions for companies to bid against each other to hire them.[19]

The demand for talent is high, and Developer Auction acts as a reputation check, selecting applications from developers with notable GitHub (a code repository) profiles and matching them against vetted startups that are looking to hire. By creating a verified playing field matching demand and supply, they're in a front-row seat to what's actually valued, which allows them to curate more and more accurately over time.

For example, if a boom in NoSQL Database Administrator hires is seen, Developer Auction will start investigating and vetting more NoSQL DB admins to meet the demand, presumably gathering feedback on who from their pool of candidates is most quickly snapped up and why. That loops back into their ability to better vet future applicants. In this way, the types of hires that get made inform the kinds of hires that Developer Auction allows to be made: The spending drives the community.

LENDING BASED ON REPUTATION

The same thing's happening with companies like Square, Simple, and Planwise—all new players in the traditional financial transaction space.[20] Square built its name with a simple dongle you plug into your iPhone's audio port which allowed you to immediately accept credit card payments. This is not only an extremely convenient way for small vendors to accept payments, but it also doesn't require a merchant account.

That's big—merchant accounts have traditionally been a huge hurdle for sellers who want to accept non-paper currencies. They require a certain credit score, years of past financial activities and details (i.e., a lot of paperwork), and particular kinds of bank accounts that are more expensive to open and maintain. What Square did was to use online information, pulling Yelp reviews, Twitter accounts, and other social platform data, to validate a company's relevant real-life existence, including how long you've been on the platform, how many reviews you have, how many followers, and so on. Square uses this to determine how many transactions a vendor should be able to make, what caps on volume to put in place, et cetera: In other words, it uses reputation to instantly make their underwriting decisions.[21]

It's only anecdotal, but it's a telling indicator (to me, at least) of how things are changing that everyone I tell about Square's validation process who is under 35 considers this completely sensible. But if you're over 60, chances seem to be good it'll make you apoplectic. Apparently there's a demographic divide in which the emerging majority thinks that mechanisms of online reputation are completely viable in evaluating financial reliability, and the exiting remainder think it's insane.

Square isn't ending there, however. Square Wallet uses your phone's ability to verify your location, and they then provide the merchant with your name and picture. You state your name, and the seller matches it against the name provided by Square and the image against the person standing in front of them attempting to execute the transaction. Simple—much simpler than using a credit card and pass code and then pretending that some scrawl on a slip of paper is any sort of useful authentication. Again, it's an example of the needs of the consumer driving the design of the transaction process.

Kabbage is another example of roughly the same thing. They provide lending to eBay sellers. It takes only ten minutes for them to run an automated online assessment of your seller account, based on past activity, history of transactions, and other information. If you pass, you can complete the application and get an advance directly into your PayPal account. All in under ten minutes. It's more narrowly defined, but otherwise is an explicit use of your online reputation to define the financial value you represent.

Again, each of these cases uses online reputation to evaluate your candidacy for lending. If you think about it, it's essentially just distributing the same mechanism used to determine a credit score, and if it's vetted by a large enough data pool, why shouldn't it be just as effective? The interesting bit is that we are already familiar with the mechanism, which makes the idea that it be used in distributed systems instead of by a singular, centralized authority seem like a natural evolution to many of us.

CORE CONSUMER COMPANIES

Simple.com is another great example in this space. It's a bank designed to have all the advantages of a "real" bank, with none of the downsides. Based on the principle that existing banks make the majority of their profits through fees and hidden charges that create an antagonistic relationship with their customers, Simple did away entirely with the concept of physical locations and focused on providing high-quality services to meet the needs of consumers. They have a credit card you can use anywhere, apps for every mobile platform, a massive ATM network, and they provide ongoing tips and budgeting tools via their extremely deep (well-developed) online platform.

In other words, they do what you would want your existing bank to do, if your existing bank was interested in your needs instead of solely in profit. And they make money completely transparently—they charge you $5 a month after six months of inactivity, and otherwise accrue interest from the margin. Interest margin is interest earned on loans minus the interest a bank pays its customers on deposits—it's the main way banks used to make money before fees proved more lucrative. Outside of that Simple makes money through interchange—revenue earned by a card-issuing bank when customers make purchases using their credit card. In this case Simple splits the interchange revenue with its bank partners.

It's not much—certainly it's much less than mainstream banks take from you. But Simple's model is significantly cheaper to run. It means that Simple is like any other bank you might use, only cheaper and more convenient, which makes it very, very easy for people to start using it as an alternative. Again, the evolution continues away from older models toward newer ones that better address our needs. That these new models are so easily integrated into reputation networks is just icing on the cake, albeit icing that's ushering us happily toward a radically different view of commerce.

It's a popular tactic. Companies using the same concept of dropping expected costs by providing services directly to customers who desire them are popping up like mushrooms after a hard rain. Gumroad.com provides an easy-to-use platform that allows you to sell anything digital, like a super-easy-to-use Google store. PaywithaTweet.com lets you give away digital goods to potential customers in exchange for tweeting about them—in essence subsidizing the marketing of the product with the product itself. I could offer a chapter from this book, for example, and you could download it for free as long as you tweeted to all your followers that you were checking it out—potentially leading to more book sales. I'm sure other permutations exist; email me (josh@josh.is), and let's figure out something to try!

Even real-life goods are seeing a shift, such as with the afore-mentioned Everland Clothing, who have no real store and make clothing based solely on member feedback. By sourcing all their materials from sources ethically correlated with the desires of their customers, they insure member buy-in (and product purchases) before they even start manufacture. Better yet, there are relatively few choices—which is actually a feature, not a bug, when you're used to the overwhelming variety of options available online.

RELEVANT TO . . . WHO?

All in all, there's a proliferation of new ways to exchange value appearing, from completely nonquantifiable gift economies to exquisitely detailed financial alternatives like Monetas, with dozens of alternatives spanning every possible mashup in between. These new models are all, in some way or another, incorporating reputation networks to provide greater value to their users while intuitively extending models of exchange we are already familiar with.

But there's a catch. Just like the drug dealer down at the playground, the first one is always free. As we get used to using these new systems, it's going to be more and more difficult to live without them; switching back to older models is going to hurt more and more. Progress only goes in one direction, and it's no longer barreling toward inventive new financial mechanisms like subprime mortgages.

So why haven't you heard more about these alternative digital currencies and time dollars and barter economies? Why aren't prediction markets all over the place? Why are meta-frameworks like Ripple only sidelines in the daily news about the economy? Obviously these things aren't mainstream, not majority enough, to be relevant, right?

The answer to that is both yes and no: The concept that they're not popular enough to warrant attention rests almost exclusively on the fact that the demographic of English-speaking, literate, well-employed, and reasonably well-educated elite is already pretty well served by traditional means like banks, loans, credit cards, and cash. They're the ones whom the majority system is designed for.

At least so far.

CHAPTER 10
A POTENTIAL TRIUMPH OF THE COMMONS

UNREGULATED DOESN'T MEAN CRIMINAL

The fact that most of the technological innovations we've described thus far hail from the First World is important, because it explains why we're so poorly equipped to estimate what will become of them. We're not the ones who are ultimately going to be using them.

Consider for a moment the scale of System D, or the black market: two-thirds of the world's working population within a decade. And recall that ancient systems like hawala—which function almost exactly like the Internet—are *thriving* within those populations. Simultaneously, all of our efforts to renovate and replace our First World systems with new technologies are revealing, again, the efficiencies and expanded value of many of the historic systems of exchange that already characterize System D. The result? We're not just building for ourselves anymore, even if we don't know it yet.

Which begs the question of how much better things are likely to be as a result of our creating radically different exchange platforms that are, on the face of things, so well fit for criminal enterprise. A big part of the answer is that systems like hawala work *because* they're unregulated, but that doesn't mean they're any more useful to criminals than existing alternatives. In fact, while it may be controversial to suggest, the opposite may be true.

A CHEAPER, LESS REGULATED SYSTEM

Before we explain why, however, it's important to recognize that one reason hawala is so appealing is because it's often a lot cheaper than routing your money through a regulated market. Outside of their commissions (which are almost always lower than banks'), hawaladars (brokers) can earn profits by bypassing official exchange rates, which is especially handy when your country happens to have an embargo or hyper-restrictive governmental regime limiting money flow. Funds often enter the system in the source country's currency and leave it in the recipient country's currency. Given that settlements frequently take place without any foreign exchange transactions, this means they can be exchanged at other than official exchange rates. (That's also a big part of the appeal of Bitcoin, by the way.)

Because these transactions are typically informal and aren't regulated by governments, they're also really helpful if you've got problems with tax or immigration. Which isn't to say it is always extralegal; in some countries hawalas are regulated by local governments, and within them hawaladars are fully licensed. In some parts of the world it's the *only* option for legitimate funds transfers, so much so that it's been used by aid organizations in areas where it works better than any alternatives.

All of which isn't great news for geopolitical entities that rely on taxation to survive and on financial regulation to control their constituents. Many government officials insist hawala can be used for money laundering, to avoid taxation, and to move wealth anonymously. And it can. Just not for the reasons typically cited by government interests.

Again, after the September 11 terrorist attacks the US government thought that some hawala brokers might have helped terrorist organizations transfer money used to fund their terrorist activities. The 9/11 Commission Report later confirmed that most of the funds used to finance the 9/11 assault weren't sent through the hawala system. Instead, they were moved using an official interbank wire transfer to a SunTrust Bank in Florida using a personal account. Let me state that in simpler terms to drive the point home: Terrorists found it easier and more secure to use an FDIC-insured bank to move the funds needed to crash a plane into the World Trade Center than an unregulated trust network comprised of their ethnic relatives.

Dr. Nikos Passas is professor of criminal justice at Northeastern University, where he specializes in the study of corruption, illicit financial/trade flows, sanctions, informal fund transfers, remittances, white collar crime, terrorism, financial regulation, organized crime, and international crimes. He is the author of "Informal Value Transfer Systems (IVTS) and Criminal Activities" (2004), "A Legislative Guide for the Implementation of the UN Convention Against Transnational Organized Crime" (2003), *International Crimes* (2003), and *Upperworld and Underworld in Cross-Border Crime* (2002). He has published more than 140 articles, book chapters, reports, and books in 13 languages; has served on the UN Monitoring Group on Taliban and *Al-Qaida* sanctions, the UN Office of Drugs and Crime, the UN Development Programme, and the World Bank; and was a team leader for a European Union Commission project on the control of proliferation/WMD finance. When it comes to international monetary transfers and extralegal exchange crime, Passas knows what he's talking about.

"I've reviewed the credit card accounts of one of the terrorists involved in the 9/11 attacks," says Passas, "and we know they used Western Union and credit card accounts through big US banks to move their funds. Law enforcement conferences, books, and articles are all obsessing over how systems like hawala or eBay are up to no good. However, these systems are all self-regulating to a large extent and in some instances offer better traceability than big Western banks."[1]

The SunTrust Bank in Florida, in contrast, was apparently not self-regulating. Instead, it was monitored by one of the richest nations of the world with one of the most advanced judiciary and regulatory banking systems on the planet. One that, coincidentally, almost collapsed along with European and Asian markets due to the subprime mortgages it was charged with regulating. But that's another story.

"If you look at terrorism cases like the Mumbai train bombings, the authorities were able to solve those cases based on information from hawala networks they were able to tap into. Those networks are actually assets, if you know where to ask the right questions," says Passas. "Hawala is largely informal, which is *why* it works effectively. It's partly that you have contacts to get into those networks, but also because of the nature of those businesses. In several nodes of the networks, brokers don't know what the ultimate destination of the money is. But they know well the immediate parties with whom they transact. That means that even if someone uses a false name to transfer the money, the broker kept books *and* knows who they passed the money to. If you follow the nodes, there is traceability. It's not transparency in terms of an electronic database, but traceability [the key objective] *is* there."

It's an interesting counterpoint to "Western banking" in which regulations are used to enforce traceability. But as Passas notes, that's no guarantee: "Where it breaks up you know you have a problem; in Western banking you have some transparency, but you may lose traceability very easily. If you use a correspondent bank account and smuggle in some transactions for a buddy of mine, who is going to find out? Even if the compliance officer wants to track you down he may not be able to. Compare that to hawala, where if you screw up nobody will do business with you again—it's self-regulating, and in some cases 'screwing up' becomes stigmatizing to a whole family or village."

Hawala systems are self-regulating in a way that no regulated banking system can be, because on an individual level there are strong, socially enforced disincentives against doing harm. For this reason, hawala systems have almost no violence related to them. After all, if you know well everyone you deal with, there are lots of good reasons not to piss anybody off or get them hurt by retributive action. In other words, hawala works using reputation.

Which doesn't mean you have to be good friends with everyone to work with hawala. "Trust has been exaggerated there; you don't have to trust them because you know if they don't deliver nobody will buy things from them ever again," says Passas. "Yes, the cultural element is indeed important; people will more easily give money to someone from the same place who speaks the same language. I'm much more likely to find someone where I drink my tea who I will give my money to than some weird guy in a suit in a bank. But these networks have become much, much larger. In the US if you don't trust a hawaladar to deliver the money it's possible to ask (for a fee) that the money be delivered first, and *then* you give the money to the local guy."

The reason I'm going on about hawala is that it's a prototypical example of a historic model, optimized for function within emergent, self-assembling, reputation-dependent networks, proliferating thanks to online systems of exchange. It's exactly what you would expect to start seeing more of as the incredibly scalable power of sensor networks, computational power, and machine learning begins to filter into the hands of the world's majority.

As point of fact, Peter Thiel—one of the founders of PayPal—just made the first European investment with his new Valar Ventures fund, putting $6 million into a company called TransferWise. What does TransferWise do? It takes the trust networks of a hawala-like system and exports them. To the web. So far they've transferred £10 million ($16 million) in 2011 (also its first year of operation), and a total of £125 million at the time of this writing. Along the way, TransferWise estimates it has saved its customers £5 million in fees.[2]

TransferWise might be the first to capitalize on the digital export of ancient systems like hawala, but it certainly won't be the last. The onlining of reputation economies is happening, and it's happening right now.

BLACK MARKET DOMINANCE

So if I can use my high Klout score for a room upgrade at the Hilton, what do I care about hawala? Wouldn't this book be more useful if I stopped talking about poor people's illegal, small-time money exchanges and got on with it?

Yes and no. Yes, because in the very short term most people in the First World probably *would* be better served learning how to game their Klout scores with astroturfing spambots (faking grass-roots efforts with programs that act like real people) or how to trick the largest number of "friends" on Facebook to like them using clever algorithms in order to sell more product.

But also, no. Firstly because that advantage is peeing in the pool for the rest of us, and secondly because—just as with Friendster—as soon as enough people get good at gaming that system it'll be replaced or obsolesced.

But more importantly because the world is about to change drastically right out from under our latte-sipping feet, regardless of our number of Twitter followers, and that change isn't going to come from the number of online views we've managed to collect or the size of our banner ads. Instead, I'm suspicious that the end of our extant global banking system's dominance will come from the much more ancient and immediate reputation networks that pervade every human system of exchange on earth—the same exact networks that currently power System D.

Again, Robert Neuwirth describes it thusly: "[System D] essentially translates as the ingenuity economy, the economy of improvisation and self-reliance, the do-it-yourself, or DIY, economy."[3]

Let that last point sink in. Does this sound at all familiar? DIY movements, an economy of improvisation and self-reliance. We've heard this before in the reshaping of the First World economy away from large-scale corporations. It's the same impetus that's given us Linux, Open Source Software, Makerbots, Etsy, Ebay, 23andMe, and more. Keep that in mind for a moment—that the defining characteristics of the global black market are starting to correlate with the most potent emerging trends of First World economies.

Originally, System D was exactly what you'd expect it would be—fruit stands by the side of the road. Taco carts under the subway line. That guy trying to pawn "his friend's stereo" out of the back of his van. In other words, it was small fish moving chump change. The only way to make "real" money was through legitimate means, a la the 9 to 5 (at best) jobs most of us have grown accustomed to in the Western world. There simply weren't any other methods of exchange that could scale System D into a meaningful alternative.

That's changed. As Neuwirth says, "In 2009, the Organisation for Economic Co-operation and Development (OECD), a think tank sponsored by the governments of 30 of the most powerful capitalist countries and dedicated to promoting free-market institutions, concluded that half the workers of the world—close to 1.8 billion people—were working in System D: off the books, in jobs that were neither registered nor regulated, getting paid in cash, and, most often, avoiding income taxes."[4]

That's *half* of the global population participating outside of the traditional economy *right now*. All relying on black market systems of exchange. Even more significantly, System D is growing. Friedrich Schneider, chair of the economics department at

Johannes Kepler University in Linz, Austria, notes that in the developing world, System D has been increasing year over year since the 1990s, and in many countries, it's growing faster than the officially recognized gross domestic product (GDP).[5] In 2009, The OECD concluded that by 2020 the shadow economy will employ *two-thirds* of the world's workers.[6] Lest you think that more than half of the world's workers are all shilling bits of mango on the street for pennies, keep in mind that according to Neuwirth's estimates, the total value of System D globally is nearly $10 *trillion*. By way of comparison, the United States has a GDP of $14 trillion. In other words, if System D were a sovereign nation, it would be the second largest economy in the world.

Scratch that. As we've already seen, just because something isn't a sovereign nation doesn't mean it isn't an economy. System D *is already* the second largest economy in the world—and it's growing significantly faster than the largest national economy in the world, the United States. Let's not fool ourselves—in many cases, this is because System D is the only option available. People from all over the world who were engaged in street selling and other kinds of unlicensed trade told Neuwirth that they could never have built their businesses in the local legal economy. "I'm totally off the grid," one unlicensed jewelry maker said. "It was never an option to do it any other way. It never even crossed my mind. It was financially absolutely impossible."

The fact that it's often the only option doesn't mean it's a bad one. System D opens markets to people who, traditionally, have been shut out of them. Rather than rolling over and dying, they're persevering in entrepreneurialism the only way they can—outside of the traditional business ecosystem. Standard economists likely consider this to be inefficient; after all, the replication of labor on a hyperlocal level is in no way utilizing all the available resources, to say nothing of minimizing loss.

But as Ronald Coase, the granddaddy of almost all modern corporate structural strategy due to his work on transaction costs (he received a Nobel Prize in economics for his work), points out, the cost of obtaining a good or service from the market is actually more than just the price of the good.[7] That "transaction cost" limits the size of an organization, and at a hyperlocal level—and increasingly on a global scale—that cost is primarily extracted by regulation and taxation.

But now that data and distribution channels are increasingly becoming free, many of those transaction costs are falling. As a result, hyperlocal labor is able to be more efficient while avoiding regulatory costs.

A side effect of stepping outside of these regulatory costs is that it lets more people participate and allows competition to flourish, thus keeping an enormous number of people employed as well as giving them an opportunity to grow their businesses where they never could have before. In other words, it creates a free market where one could not previously exist.

Neuwirth notes: "In São Paulo, Ãdison Ramos Dattora, a migrant from the rural midlands, has succeeded in the nation's commercial capital by working as a camelô—an unlicensed street vendor. He started out selling candies and chocolates on the trains, and is now in a more lucrative branch of the street trade—retailing pirate DVDs of first-run movies to commuters around downtown. His underground trade—he has to watch out for the cops wherever he goes—has given his family a standard of living he never dreamed possible: a bank account, a credit card, an apartment in the center of town, and enough money to take a trip to Europe."[8]

System D is more than just a liberated version of existing, "legitimate" markets. It's also a significant financial coping mechanism where the regulated economy cannot be sustained (as is increasingly the case in the disrupted economies of the First and Second

Worlds). That's important as the costs of the regulated economy are getting higher at the same time that new means of exchange—like Square, Simple, Bitcoin, or Ripple—are emerging with less cost, easier regulation, and wider access. In other words, a massive market for these new platforms already exists, with increasing regulatory costs driving a growing desire for alternatives. Lest you are tempted to write this off as a Third World phenomena, keep in mind how close the United States was to financial collapse with the subprime mortgage crisis or the fiscal cliff debacle.

Even more importantly, it appears that System D may create significant resilience to financial downturns. A study by Deutsche Bank (the huge German commercial lender) in 2009 indicated that people in the European countries with the largest unlicensed and unregulated portions of their economies—those with the most System D—survived the economic meltdown of 2008 better than folks living in tightly regulated, centrally planned nations.[9] By way of example, studies of countries throughout Latin America showed that people turned almost exclusively to System D to survive the most recent financial crisis there.[10]

In this way System D can help counter the effects of recession on the formal economy. "When wages go down, there is more incentive to move towards the black economy. It is almost a form of insurance, a way out," says Pietro Reichlin, economics professor at Rome's Luiss university.[11] Friedrich Schneider agrees. It's "welfare-enhancing," he says. "Without the shadow economy, Spain would collapse. It's the only part of the economy that keeps the economy alive. You immediately get cash, you immediately earn something to feed your family."

Somalia is perhaps the last place you'd expect to hear tales of economic prosperity. But it's actually a great example of how informal economies can not only sustain but support a growing economy. According to the CIA and the Central Bank of Somalia, despite experiencing civil unrest, Somalia has developed a very healthy informal economy. It's not just based on livestock and fruitstands, either, but also on money transfer companies and telecommunications.

Because of a lack of formal government statistics (not to mention the recent civil war), it's hard to quantify the size or growth of that economy, but for 2009 the CIA estimated that the GDP was up to $5.731 billion, with a projected real growth rate of 2.6 percent, from a GDP estimate of $3.3 billion in 1994.[12]

According to a 2007 British Chambers of Commerce report: "The private sector also grew, particularly in the service sector. Unlike the pre–civil war period when most services and the industrial sector were government-run, there has been substantial, albeit unmeasured, private investment in commercial activities; this has been largely financed by the Somali diaspora, and includes trade and marketing, money transfer services, transportation, communications, fishery equipment, airlines, telecommunications, education, health, construction and hotels."[13]

Somalia is also a great example of why System D isn't necessarily a utopian solution to all our woes. For one thing, unregulated economies *aren't regulated*, which has some big downsides, such as faked medicine, unsafe foods, slave labor, robbery, and similar negative side effects of nobody being in a position of power to stop the perpetrators. It's not for nothing that Somalia is becoming synonymous with "Pirates."

Beyond a lack of controls to stop fraud, unsafe business practices, and exploitation, it's also often very harmful to the legitimate economy. In many places people just don't report that they're working and go on collecting unemployment benefits in addition to working on the black market. That's extraordinarily common in places like Spain, where it is widely accepted that the Spanish jobless rate of double the European average is a fiction.

As an example, when Spanish "unemployment fell to 8.5 per cent at the height of the boom in 2006–07, a huge number of employers complained they could find no workers to hire"; but at the same time that unemployment rate (which is, coincidentally, a Spanish minimum in recent history) is so high that it would be considered a deep economic recession in any other industrialized country. Instead, it appears to be business as usual in Spain.[14] The general opinion appears to be that nobody is paying social security contributions, but everyone is cashing them out.

THE RICH/POOR DIVIDE

Before you rush in to condemn these unsafe, black market practices by the global 99 percent, consider the state of affairs in legitimate markets. According to a new report released by international rights group and charity Oxfam, closing tax havens maintained by the rich and wealthy could yield as much as $189 *billion* in tax revenues. Oxfam's figures indicated that as much as $32 *trillion* is currently stored in tax havens.[15]

So it's not just the black market that's avoiding paying taxes. Nor is it only the black market that's avoiding regulation; China (the country) was recently accused of causing a nationwide crisis in Tanzania and Uganda by allowing its factories to sell fake malaria pills to the point that *one in every three* pills available in those countries was simply useless.[16]

Really, the most significant difference between highly regulated formal economies and System D appears to be that the legitimate market has to date been more successful at aggregating wealth in the hands of the few through meeting the minimum demands of the many. According to Oxfam, the incomes of the richest 1 percent in the world have grown by 60 percent over the last 20 years, with the latest world financial crisis hastening, rather than hindering, the process. The result is that the world's 100 richest people earned enough money last year ($240 billion net income) to end extreme poverty four times over.[17]

In fact, there's a fair amount of evidence that the people of the First World are following trends seen in Third World nations in which the population is split purely into the rich and the non-rich—the demise of the middle class that so many have written about. Right now, it seems as though that middle class is the only group paying taxes and buying into existing First World financial systems, with the result that they're poorer, have less economic opportunity, and suffer higher unemployment.

It begs the question of which is the lesser evil: completely unregulated black market networks, or highly centralized financial oligarchies. Both have costs and advantages. But right now, the pendulum is swinging away from the banks and existing financial power elite, backed by a runaway train of technology developers, emerging social platform adherents, and an underserved global majority.

As an early-stage case in point, earlier this year Megaupload.com, one of the largest file sharing sites in the world, was reborn as "Mega.com" exactly one year after it was shut down by a raid from the FBI. Megaupload was widely lauded as *the* place to go to illegally download films, books, porn, etc. Kim Dotcom, the founder, decided to found the new iteration not in Panama, or in a shady back-lot office in the Cayman Islands, but in New Zealand, where copyright offenses alone are not enough to warrant extradition. In other words, he's launching the service where the laws are most in his favor, and that place happens to be a respected First World country. This time he's launching Mega using military-grade encryption, set up as a security-oriented, high-privacy cloud storage service. In other words, it'll serve the same function as Megaupload, only evolved to prevent the takedown attempts that were launched against its predecessor.

It's a classic story of Internet architecture, in which censorship is seen as damage and routed around. Except this time it's also making use of a shifting world stage in which significant governmental entities are starting to recognize that the rules of the game are changing and are hedging their bets accordingly.

If this is already beginning to happen in countries like New Zealand, how is the shakeup going to affect individuals? Most people aren't going to be able to jump ship to another country just to take advantage of tax or IP legislation. What happens when those people instead start looking for solutions they can actually use, like moving over to System D or its digital equivalents?

DESIGNING FOR REPUTATION, NOT JUST FINANCE

Consider where we started in this book, with the massive uptick in computational power, data aggregation, and machine intelligence that's currently being exploited by corporate interests. That same capability is increasingly finding its way into the hands of small, self-aggregating, socially oriented individuals at the same time as roughly *half of the world's workforce* is using alternative means of finance. System D is happening because the existing financial system *isn't working* for the nonrich, and the nonrich are a growing class that increasingly includes the folks developing the software.

If code is culture, this means we're looking at an international shift of tectonic proportions. That's because the platforms that are being developed now are, deliberately or accidentally, *being made for System D*. Uber's car service could easily move to taking Bitcoin, or hawala payments, or Klout score bonuses with just a few lines of code. Skillshare could incorporate Maltego to allow alternative payment means, or roll up a time banking scheme to encourage local economies to improve their on-the-ground user base and communities. Google, for that matter, could use its universal login methods to help network a variety of these schemes to make its payment platform, Google Checkout, suddenly global and increasingly outside of US financial regulations.

If (or I should say *when*) they do, all these organizations suddenly have the opportunity to massively expand their market share. Right now most of us in the First World are enamored with our status as the technological elite—look at all these new ways to post pictures from my iPhone! See all the *Angry Birds* apps I have! Check out these hip new glasses I got through my fashion blog! But along the way we may have forgotten that we're only the very tip of the iceberg. The Internet is big, but in terms of its likely impact on world history, it's only just getting started.

THE SECOND AND THIRD WORLD BOOM

Forgive me for repeating myself, but these numbers are significant: Only 34.3 percent of the world has Internet access, an amount that has gone up 566.4 percent in slightly more than a decade.[18] Mobile phones are the fastest-growing segment of that, and 80 percent of the world has a mobile phone right now. That said, out of the 5 billion mobile phones in the world, only 1.08 billion are smartphones that offer connectivity with the Internet.[19] More than 50 percent of the smartphone penetration is in developed markets, with less than 20 percent in emerging markets.[20]

That means that the markets most likely to use our new reputation-based social networks and methods of exchange *haven't even arrived yet*. Roughly two-thirds of the planet is about to hop online all at once over the next 5 to 20 years, with all the same technological capacity and capability that we have in the first world, and when they do they're going to find a bevy of systems of exchange waiting for them that look very familiar. They just won't be the ones we've built our First World economies on.

Which is actually pretty good timing. The existing financial markets in the First World are destabilizing, and people are starting to notice. As they do, new technological alternatives are falling into their hands, allowing them to make better and more powerful reputation economies—systems of exchange that are abundance-oriented and meritocratic, instead of artificially constrained and elitist. Concurrent to all of this the second-biggest economy in the world—the participants in System D—are about to come online to join the game.

RISK AND OPPORTUNITY

The result is an opportunity of truly epic proportions. For one thing, a hell of a lot of good could come of this: For the first time in human history we have the possibility of utterly changing how commerce is done, potentially turning regional inequality into a global meritocratic marketplace.

If everyone on the planet can access free education and open markets on which to trade according to performance—not race, religion, or region—we could see a complete redistribution of industry and wealth following first principles of universal benefit. Decentralization of resources through gift economies, barter, and trade could destroy world hunger (we already know we have enough food for everyone; it's just not well distributed yet) and unemployment. Pollyannic as it sounds, we could shift from global scarcity—with all the intolerance, exploitation, and suffering that entails—to a worldwide market of abundance.

On the other hand, we could also see an unprecedented descent into global chaos. Online anonymity and unequal access to technology could allow organized crime to more effectively compete with governments, while those same governments could suddenly find their tax base vanishing into circumvention technologies.

An influx of unregulated medicines, foods, and services could lead to or exacerbate problems from pandemics to poisonings. A spooked set of governments and industries could enforce nation-wide police states as they attempt to maintain the status quo. Empowered, anonymous individuals could launch increasingly sophisticated cyber-attacks, leading to more generalized chaos. In other words, we don't know what's going to happen—but the implications are huge.

So what to do? For a start, it's time to take the tools and techniques we have at hand and begin trying to use them in a new way. Rather than always maximizing for profit, reputation economics asks us to analyze our systems in light of maximum *benefit*. The distinction is difficult; it requires we think contextually. It muddies the waters with relativism, social good, and a global breadth of scale. It forces us to assume, in many ways, moral responsibility for what we are making, with the upside that we can benefit more from benefiting others.

The alternative is a hastening of the serious problems we're already facing as a species—environmental, cultural, and commercial problems of often irreversible scope. Your new marketing campaign won't cause global warming to happen all at once, but it could certainly quicken its progress. Conversely, it could foster a new social good which simultaneously makes your product more appealing and your organization more profitable. Reputation economics makes the analysis harder, but the outcomes more valuable.

WELCOME TO THE NEW REPUTATION ECONOMY

We are at the start of a global shift in how humanity approaches its next several hundred years of commerce. Code is culture; the platforms we're writing now will set the tone for the emerging markets that are about to join the game all over the world. If we can instantiate systems now, here, that allow for multiple kinds of value to be exchanged—meaning that we're all richer and better able to obtain value in return—we'll have made a fundamental leap forward in what commerce can be for everyone. The platforms we make, the standards we choose, and the values we code into them could allow for meritocracies to emerge that can be globally inclusive and communally beneficial. That simply hasn't been possible before in the history of the human race.

It certainly won't be easy. Existing geopolitical entities depend on finance as it functions now and won't want to give up the power and wealth built into current systems. Large-scale multinationals may decide it makes better financial sense to fight to maintain the status quo than to risk evolution into the new economy.

Unfortunately for them those fights are by definition limited by geography, and this new world we live in just isn't anymore. Want to prohibit me from using Bitcoin here in the United States? OK, I'll host my site in Sweden, convert ownership to my double Irish with a Dutch sandwich shell corp (that I bought online from a site in Moldova), and then spend that bitcoin as dollars through a Simple bank card. And I'll do it all from Michigan, because I like the fishing here, and you can just get along somehow without my income being taxed, thanks very much.

In the same way, existing financial and commercial systems that aren't fulfilling the needs of the markets that seek to use them will have to evolve—or be replaced. That's mostly because they aren't the only option anymore. Multiplier markets that use intuitive markers like reputation are growing, and platforms to sustain them are developing fast just as the majority of customers who want to use them are starting to flock to the world stage. As they do, the winners will be those who get most adept at providing the most value using these new methods.

The silver lining to all this disruptive change is that the responsibility rests on all of us together. No one individual is likely to stand up and replace the global economy en masse. Instead, reputation economics asks us each to act in our own best interest, simultaneously with the interests of others. By changing our businesses and ourselves to obtain maximum benefit from abundance economies and meritocracies, we both profit more and make the world better.

As the world changes, radically and quickly, we're all going to be forced to transition. The faster we do it, the more we stand to gain. The question is no longer if you will join...it's when.

I'll see you there.

Joshua Klein / josh@josh.is / @joshuaklein
July 30, 2013, New York City

NOTES

CHAPTER 1

1. Charles Duhigg, "How Companies Learn Your Secrets," *New York Times Magazine*, February 16, 2012, nyti.ms/12QrGGw.
2. Ibid.
3. "Internet Usage Statistics: The Internet Big Picture," *Internet World Stats*, accessed July 1, 2013, bit.ly/10WA61D.
4. Helena, "How Many People Use Smartphones in the World," *Onbile*, accessed July 1, 2013, bit.ly/15HQzIz.
5. Sarah Perez, "It's Still A Feature Phone World: Global Smartphone Penetration At 27%," *Techcrunch*, accessed August 12, 2013, tcrn.ch/15ydeEW.

CHAPTER 2

1. David Graeber, *Debt: The First 5,000 Years* (New York: Melville House 2011).
2. Don Tapscott, interview with author, January 14, 2013.
3. "Commerce," Wikipedia, accessed August 12, 2013, bit.ly/12Y17vj.
4. David Frum, "What Really Went Wrong with the Nixon Shock? (Updated)," *Frum Forum*, August 15, 2011, bit.ly/1bGOfqC.
5. "System D: The Shadow Economy Is the Second Largest in the World," *Freakonomics,* November 1, 2011, bit.ly/17fyA9M.
6. Robert Neuwirth, "The Shadow Superpower," *Foreign Policy*, October 28, 2011, atfp.co/11QWdZL.
7. Chris Prentice, "Shadow Economies on the Rise Around the World," *Bloomberg Businessweek*, July 29, 2010, buswk.co/12DY2TP.
8. "Hawala," *Wikipedia*, accessed July 1, 2013, bit.ly/12s16n8

CHAPTER 3

1. Blake Ellis, "Average Student Loan Debt Nears $27,000," *CNN Money*, October 18, 2012, cnnmon.ie/13lLDns.
2. Hope Yen, "US Poverty on Track to Rise to Highest Since 1960s," *Associated Press,* July 23, 2012, yhoo.it/13lLHUr.

3. Anya Kamenetz, interview with author, December 5, 2012.
4. Marina Gorbis, interview with author, December 12, 2012.
5. Sunny Bates, interview with author, December 11, 2012.
6. David Brodwin, "The Rise of the Collaborative Consumption Economy," *US News & World Report*, August 9, 2012, bit.ly/145jl7h.
7. Michael Arrington, "The Moment of Truth for Airbnb as User's Home Is Utterly Trashed," *TechCrunch*, July 27, 2011, tcrn.ch/13dYgW4.
8. Travis, "Uber Policy White Paper 1.0," *Uber,*. April 12, 2013, bit.ly/1e9iCSq.
9. Clay Shirky, interview with author, December 17, 2012.

CHAPTER 4

1. Matt Grainger, "40% of Social Network Accounts Are Spammers," *PCR*, May 30, 2012, bit.ly/13dYo86.
2. Happy Rockefeller, "The HB Gary Email That Should Concern Us All," *Daily Kos*, February 16, 2011, bit.ly/12QsQBI.
3. Jeremiah Owyang, "Brands Start Automating Social Media Responses on Facebook and Twitter," *TechCrunch*, June 7, 2012, tcrn.ch/1dA3OvU.
4. Bre Pettis, interview with author, December 20, 2012.
5. Rebecca J. Rosen, "The Missing 20th Century: How Copyright Protection Makes Books Vanish," *The Atlantic*, March 30, 2012, bit.ly/16hMQSm.
6. Ibid.
7. Cory Doctorow, "Why the Entertainment Industry's Release Strategy Creates Piracy," *Guardian*, December 20, 2012. bit.ly/18jFy46.
8. Ibid.
9. Ibid.
10. Mike Masnick, "Nathan Myhrvold's Intellectual Ventures Using Over 1,000 Shell Companies To Hide Patent Shakedown," *Techdirt,* February 18, 2010, bit.ly/13Xrd91.
11. Adam Ludwig and Adrienne Burke, "GE-Quirky Deal Opens Tech Patents to Almost Everybody," *Techonomy*, April 10, 2013, bit.ly/12s1Jx4.
12. Cory Doctorow, "RIAA Bigwig Who Architected Anti-technology Lawsuits Is Now #2 at the Copyright Office," *Boing Boing*, January 31, 2013, bit.ly/15yfbS3.
13. "Esther Dyson," *Wikipedia*, accessed July 3, 2013, bit.ly/13dYQmO.
14. Esther Dyson, interview with author, January 3, 2013.
15. Ibid.
16. Bianca Bosker, "Google CEO On Privacy (VIDEO): 'If You Have Something You Don't Want Anyone To Know, Maybe You Shouldn't Be Doing It,'" *Huffington Post*, March 18, 2010, huff.to/13l8l5V.
17. "Happy Birthday, Facebook Disconnect," *Disconnect*, October 21, 2011, bit.ly/17aKlxx.
18. Alexia Tsotsis, "Former Googler Launches Disconnect, Browser Extension That Disables Third Party Data Tracking," *TechCrunch*, December 13, 2010, tcrn.ch/15u025J.
19. Zach Epstein, "Non-profit ISP wages war on FBI and DOJ by Putting Privacy First [video]," *BGR*, April 12, 2012, bit.ly/11sYXdE.
20. "About," *Sopatrack*, bit.ly/16AwAdh.

CHAPTER 5

1. Cory Doctorow, "City Buses Across America Now Covertly Recording Passengers' Conversations," *Boing Boing*, December 13, 2012, bit.ly /1bgVdkV.
2. Anonymous, "Hidden Government Scanners Will Instantly Know Everything About You from 164 Feet Away," *Gizmodo*, July 10, 2012, bit .ly/13KKXj7.
3. "Skype with Care: Microsoft Is Reading Everything You Write," The H Security, May 14, 2013, bit.ly/15yfTyu.
4. Zachary M. Seward, "What Bloomberg Employees Can See When They Snoop on Customers," *Quartz*, May 10, 2013, bit.ly/12DZOUZ.
5. David Kravets, "Biometric Database of All Adult Americans Hidden in Immigration Reform," *Wired*, May 10, 2013, bit.ly/11QXYGx.
6. John Gilmore, "John Gilmore, Entrepreneur and Civil Libertarian," *Toad*, March 25, 2011, bit.ly/13kJo95.
7. Joseph Walker, "Meet the New Boss: Big Data," *The Wall Street Journal*, September 20, 2012, on.wsj.com/13dZYqC.
8. Ibid.
9. Brian Christian, "The A/B Test: Inside the Technology That's Changing the Rules of Business," *Wired*, April 25, 2012, bit.ly/13KLilV.
10. "Machine Learning," *Wikipedia*, accessed August 12, 2013, bit.ly/1a9xF22.
11. "Bayes Theorum," *Wikipedia*, accessed July 30, 2013, bit.ly/13vp01e.
12. Ibid.
13. Ibid.

CHAPTER 6

1. Marshall Kirkpatrick, "When Bots Go Mad," *Read Write Web*, February 25, 2012, rww.to/10WBD7H.
2. Ibid.
3. "Dictionary + Algorithm + PoD T-shirt Printer + Lucrative Meme = Rape T-shirts on Amazon," *I am Pete Ashton*, March 2, 2013, bit.ly/18gPxUr.
4. "CDC: Use Anti-viral Medication for Flu," *UPI*, January 10, 2013, bit.ly /1ebedyp.
5. Nick Bilton, "Disruptions: Data Without Context Tells a Misleading Story," Bits: New York Times tech blog, February 24, 2013, nyti.ms/18jGw0i.
6. P. Gosselin, "Mathematical Computer Models Fail Utterly in the Search for the Wreckage of Air France Flight 447," *NoTricksZone*, May 3, 2011, bit. ly/1ao3lgp.
7. "Computer Models Utterly Fail to Predict Climate Changes," *Wintery Knight*, June 15, 2012, bit.ly/18gPK9Z.
8. Ross McKitrick, "Junk Science Week: Climate Models Fail Reality Test," *Financial Post*, December 6, 2013, bit.ly/14D137E.
9. Ibid.
10. Ibid.
11. Amaranth, Hedge funds, "Amaranth Weekend / Morning Headline Roundup," *Wall Street Folly*, September 25, 2006, bit.ly/14ivSp1.

12. "U.S. Commodity Futures Trading Commission Charges Hedge Fund Amaranth and its Former Head Energy Trader, Brian Hunter, with Attempted Manipulation of the Price of Natural Gas Futures," *US Commodity Futures Trading Commission*, July 25, 2007, 1.usa.gov/1ebf95W.

13. David H. Freedman, "Why Economic Models Are Always Wrong," *Scientific American*, October 26, 2011, bit.ly/1bCOKiV.

14. Ibid.

15. Ewen Callaway, "Economics and Genetics Meet in Uneasy Union," *Nature*, October 10, 2012, bit.ly/15vzmRU.

16. Ibid.

17. Joseph Walker, "Meet the New Boss: Big Data," *Wall Street Journal*, September 20, 2012, on.wsj.com/13dZYqC.

18. Seth Stevenson, "What Your Klout Score Really Means," *Wired*, April 24, 2012, bit.ly/16EkHBH.

19. Ibid.

20. John Melloy, "Mysterious Algorithm Was 4% of Trading Activity Last Week," *CNBC*, October 8, 2012, cnb.cx/13zw0t6.

21. "Strong AI," *Wikipedia*, accessed July 30, 2013, bit.ly/15vzReW.

22. Ibid.

23. "Intelligence amplification," *Wikipedia*, accessed July 30, 2013, bit.ly /18MSUCF.

24. "Codify," *Oxford Dictionaries*, accessed July 30, 2013, bit.ly/132TibI.

25. Ann Finkbeiner, "Searching for Jim Gray," *Last Word on Nothing*, March 17, 2011, bit.ly/18YxlBR.

CHAPTER 7

1. Adrienne Burke, "Next Trick for Laser Printers: Manufacturing Electronics," *Techonomy*, April 9, 2013, bit.ly/15HTgdb.

2. Katia Moskvitch, "Modern Meadow Aims to Print Raw Meat Using Bioprinter," *BBC News*, January 21, 2013, bbc.in/1bCP6pC.

3. Adriana Lee, "After 3D Printable Gun Bans, Pirate Bay Steps in to Distribute Plans," *TechnoBuffalo*, May 11, 2013, tchno.be/12s32Mt.

4. Colin Grant, "3D-Printed Canal Home Takes Shape in Amsterdam," *BBC News*, April 15, 2013, bbc.in/18jHhq6.

5. "Pretty Small Things," *Thingiverse*, accessed August 12, 2013, bit.ly /14NzWvA.

6. John Markoff, "Skilled Work, Without the Worker," *New York Times*, August 18, 2012, nyti.ms/18gQjRf.

7. Ibid.

8. Ibid.

9. Ibid.

10. Yearly Box Office Report, *Box Office Mojo*, accessed July 10, 2013, bit.ly /145nvMp.

11. "Pirates? Hollywood Sets $10+ Billion Box Office Record," *Torrent Freak*, December 31, 2012, bit.ly/10WCjKc.

12. Greg Sandoval, "RIAA: Consumers Are Shelling Out for Subscription Music," *CNET*, March 27, 2012, cnet.co/17gcxSe.

CHAPTER 8

1. Colleen Taylor, "Airbnb Hits Hockey Stick Growth: 10 Million Nights Booked, 200K Properties," *TechCrunch*, June 19, 2012, tcrn.ch/1ao4chg.
2. Rob Trump, "Why Would You Ever Give Money Through Kickstarter?" *The New York Times*, February 8, 2013, nyti.ms/17iTbtQ.
3. Sarah Mitroff, "Kickstarter Campaigns Reap $319M in 2012," *Wired*, January 9, 2013, bit.ly/17gcHcn.
4. Ross Kenneth Urken, "Are Bitcoins Becoming Europe's New Safe Haven Currency," *DailyFinance*, April 8, 2013, aol.it/12AZye8.
5. Max Raskin, "Dollar-Less Iranians Discover Virtual Currency," *Bloomberg Businessweek*, November 29, 2012, buswk.co/1bCQ7y9.
6. "Guidance: Application of FinCEN's Regulations to Persons Administering, Exchanging, or Using Virtual Currencies," *Financial Crimes Enforcement Network*, March 18, 2013, 1.usa.gov/12s3tX3.
7. Tom Watson, "Olympics Coverage: NBC Apparently Thinks It's 1992, Seemingly Unaware of Twitter's Existence," *Forbes*, July 27, 2012, onforb.es/13KMzcD.

CHAPTER 9

1. Black Duck Software, "The 2012 Future of Open Source Survey Results," *SlideShare*, May 21, 2012, slidesha.re/12s3z0T.
2. Tim Yeaton, "The Future of Open Source Annual Survey Results Reveal Important Insights Challenges," *OpenSource Delivers*, May 21, 2012, bit.ly /12AZQBy.
3. "How Do Big US Firms Use Open Source Software?" *Blog dds*, March 22, 2012, bit.ly/15HUllo.
4. "Attribution-Commercial-ShareAlike 3.0 Unported" license agreement, *Creative Commons*, accessed July 10, 2013, bit.ly/15g3K1s.
5. Marina Gorbis, interview with author, December 12, 2012.
6. "For Spain's Jobless, Time Equals Money," *Wall Street Journal*, August 27, 2012, on.wsj.com/12s3ESl.
7. "La Sonrisa, Una Moneda Social Que Ayuda A Escolares EN Avila Y Que EN Estados Unidos Protege Al Comercio Local," *Vivir sin Empleo*, September 5, 2013, bit.ly/15yjJb1.
8. Ibid.
9. "Ripple (monetary system)," *Wikipedia*, accessed July 10, 2013, bit.ly /14U7SVO.
10. Julia Dixon, "Powered by Monetas," *DGC Magazine*, December 10, 2012, bit.ly/15g414g.
11. Romain Dillet, "Clothing Store Startup Everlane Opens a Pop-up Store in New York, Now Has 400,000 Active Members," *TechCrunch*, December 13, 2012, tcrn.ch/14U8w5T.
12. "Prediction Market," *Wikipedia*, accessed July 10, 2013, bit.ly/12s3NoM.
13. "Patri Friedman," *Wikipedia*, accessed August 12, 2013, bit.ly/15yk7q2.
14. "Robin Hanson," *Wikipedia*, accessed on August 12, 2013, bit.ly/11R0ufY.
15. Tim Sullivan, interview with author, July 25, 2013.

16. Justin Wolfers, "Prediction Markets in Science," *Freakonomics*, May 16, 2008, bit.ly/1dA6OrX.
17. Ken Howery, interview with author, December 19, 2012.
18. Ibid.
19. Billy Gallagher, "Quora, DropBox, Others Made $30M in Job Offers to Engineers in First 2 Weeks of Developer Auction," *TechCrunch*, September 6, 2012, tcrn.ch/14U8haZ.
20. Joel Falconer, "The Future of Money: New Pardigms for the Checkout, Banking & Currency," *Next Web*, December 9, 2012, tnw.co/16Emy9G.
21. "Social Media Relevancy Is the New Credit Score," *TekFin*, October 1, 2010, bit.ly/12s44YL.

CHAPTER 10

1. Nikos Passas, interview with author, December 10, 2012.
2. Leo Mirani, "Facebook's First Funder Just Backed TransferWise, a Startup That's Like an Ancient Islamic Money Transfer System," *Quartz*, May 14, 2013, bit.ly/13lTx08.
3. Robert Neuwirth, "The Shadow Superpower," *Foreign Policy*, October 28, 2011, atfp.co/11R0Y5I.
4. Ibid.
5. Friedrich Schneider, "Shadow Economies and Corruption All Over the World: New Estimates for 145 Countries," July 2007, bit.ly/11R14dx.
6. Marco Rabinowitz, "Rise of the Shadow Economy: Second Largest Economy in the World," *Forbes*, November 7, 2011, onforb.es/10WDrxz.
7. "Ronald Coase," Wikipedia, accessed July 30, 2013, bit.ly/14DM2T8.
8. Robert Neuwirth, "The Shadow Superpower," *Foreign Policy*, October 28, 2011, atfp.co/11QWdZL.
9. Deutsche Bank Research, "Shadow Economy Defies Crisis—Year-end Note with a Wry Pitch," December 21, 2009, bit.ly/14Ud8ZF.
10. "Europe's 'Black Economy,'" *Impact Lab*, July 2, 2011, bit.ly/10WGhTi.
11. Ibid.
12. "Economy of Somalia," *Wikipedia*, accessed July 10, 2013, bit.ly/16ErAmB.
13. Ibid.
14. "Europe's 'Black Economy,'" *Impact Lab*.
15. "The Cost of Inequality: How Wealth and Income Extremes Hurt Us All," *Oxfam Media*, January 18, 2013, bit.ly/12s7Wce.
16. Kathleen E. McLaughlin, "China's Aid in Africa: Good Intentions Mix with Bad Drugs," *Pulitzer Center on Crisis Reporting*, December 21, 2012, bit.ly/10WGnu7.
17. "The Cost of Inequality: How Wealth and Income Extremes Hurt Us All," *Oxfam Media*.
18. "Internet Usage Statistics: The Internet Big Picture," *Internet World Stats*, accessed July 1, 2013, bit.ly/10WA61D.
19. Helena, "How Many People Use Smartphones in the World," *Onbile*, accessed July 1, 2013, bit.ly/15HQzIz.
20. Sarah Perez, "It's Still a Feature Phone World: Global Smartphone Penetration At 27%," *Techcrunch*, accessed August 12, 2013, tcrn.ch /15ydeEW.

INDEX